A Guide to the World of Cycling

Other books by Paul McCallum:
The Downhill Skiing Handbook (with Christine Lariviere McCallum)
A Practical Self-Defense Guide for Women
The Scuba Diving Handbook
Underwater Adventures

SPINNING
A Guide to the World of Cycling

Paul McCallum

BETTERWAY BOOKS
CINCINNATI, OHIO

Cover design by Rick Britton
Typography by Park Lane Associates

NOTE TO THE READER: Although some of the people featured in this book are not wearing helmets for reasons of photographic vanity, I do not condone or encourage cycling without a helmet. For your safety, *always wear a helmet when riding a bike*.

Spinning. Copyright © 1993 by Paul McCallum. Printed and bound in the United States of America. All rights reserved. No part of this book may be reproduced in any form or by any electronic or mechanical means including information storage and retrieval systems without permission in writing from the publisher, except by a reviewer, who may quote brief passages in a review. Published by Betterway Books, an imprint of F&W Publications, Inc., 1507 Dana Avenue, Cincinnati, Ohio 45207. 1-800-289-0963. First edition.

---

97 96 95 94 93   5 4 3 2 1

Library of Congress Cataloging-in-Publication Data
McCallum, Paul
    Spinning : a guide to the world of cycling / Paul McCallum. — 1st ed.
      p. cm.
    Includes index.
    ISBN 1-55870-286-5 : $14.95
    1. Cycling. 2. Bicycles. I. Title.
GV1041.M38 1993
796.6--dc20
                                                                       92-38568
                                                                              CIP

*This book is Dedicated to
Charlie,
Thank you for everything.*

Acknowledgments

Thanks to everyone from our Saturday morning rides ... Chipper, Michael King, Tom and Sharon Maney, Christine, Jay O'Donnel, Larry Jacobson, Michel and Sylvie Lariviere ... all of you have made it fun!

Thanks also to:

Kelly Maney—For her excellent proofreading of the original manuscript.

Josh Bertram — For hopping, jumping, and contorting his mountain bike for "just one more picture."

Tom Maney—For getting me back into cycling.

Sharon Maney—For letting Tom go riding.

Celia Jensen — For her help in the preparation of this manuscript.

Ann Mania—For her input on touring and bicycle maintenance.

Quiggle—For showing us how to fall.

Rick Denman—For his input on velodrome racing.

The cyclists at the Encino Velodrome.

Susie Dotan—For all her help and advice.

Bob Hostage and the staff of Betterway Books—For their continuing support.

Christine McCallum—For everything!

Contents

1. Cycling Into the 21st Century 11
    Why You Should Ride a Bike
    The History of Cycling

2. The Bike 21
    Choosing the Right Equipment ... Cost
    Anatomy of a Bicycle ... Types of Bikes
    What Bike Should You Buy? ... Saddles
    Shifting Systems ... Brakes ... Pedals ... Tires

3. Accessories and Custom Equipment 39
    Computers ... Clothing ... Water Bottles
    Tire Pumps ... Lightweight Parts
    Heart Monitors ... Rollers and Stationary Trainers
    Locks ... Lights ... Rock Shox Suspension
    Protective Gear ... Bike Racks and Boxes
    Children's Seats and Trailers ... Aerobars

4. Safety 57
    Helmets ... Eyewear ... Reflective Equipment
    Lights ... Protective Pads and Clothing
    Rearview Mirror ... How to Ride Safely

5. Bike Handling Skills 67
    Off-Road Riding Skills ... Road Bike Skills

6. Training 81
    Starting Out: Your First Rides
    The Importance of Warming Up ... Intensity
    Spinning ... Cadence ... Lactic Acid
    Heart Rate ... Aerobic Training

Intervals and Sprinting ... Pacelines ... Rest
Recovery Rides ... Endurance
Don't Be Redundant in Your Training
Training for the Peloton ... Set Goals
Breathing

7. Racing 97

Wind Resistance/Drafting ... The Start of a Race
Preview the Course ... Dealing with Fear
Velodrome Racing ... Road Racing
Off-Road Racing ... The Race Across America

8. Cycling Health and Diet 113

The Importance of Water ... Losing Weight
Back Problems ... Numb Hands ... Numb Feet
Knee Pain ... Hygiene ... Saddle Sores
Nature's Hazards ... Diet

9. Maintenance and Repair 127

Tools ... Fixing a Flat Tire
Derailleur Problems ... Steering Problems
Adjusting the Hubs ... Spokes
Adjusting the Bottom Bracket ... Brake Problems
Finish Line Products

10. Touring 145

Types of Tours ... Selecting a Tour
Should You Rent a Bike? ... Have Fun on the Trip
Pace Yourself ... What You Should Bring
Tools and Spare Parts ... Travel Insurance
The PAC Tour

11. Publications and Organizations 161

GLOSSARY 167

INDEX 171

1
Cycling Into the 21st Century

Riding a bike will turn you into a perfect person and enable you to get everything you want out of life. Perhaps a slight overstatement, but no matter what your current situation—good or bad—riding a bike will improve the quality of your life!

WHY YOU SHOULD RIDE A BIKE

There are a lot of reasons this is true, but the fact that cycling is such an easy, extremely fun, stress-free form of exercise is the foundation of all its benefits; there are many. At the very least, your heart will become stronger and your cardiovascular system will improve. In fact, some people's hearts actually slightly increase in size after following an exercise program and thus become capable of pumping more blood. The result is that you have more energy than a sedentary person since the muscles are getting more oxygen with every heartbeat.

Starting a cycling program is easy and won't stress your body. Unlike some exercises, such as running, which can jar your body into damage, cycling won't hurt you. If you're overweight, cycling may be an ideal sport for you to get into since it is relatively stress-free on your joints. The gearing on modern bikes allows you to avoid straining your knees, and you can stay on flat terrain during your first few months of riding.

Another advantage to bike riding is that it's a fun form of exercise. Wouldn't you rather go for a bike ride in the fresh air than spend two hours in a crowded gym surrounded by sweaty people? Exercise on a bike isn't work, it's fun!

The fact that cycling can be an extremely social activity adds to its appeal. According to a recent survey in *Bicycling* magazine, there are approximately 82.6 million adult cyclists in the United States, and that number is increasing by about five percent every year. Clearly, you will be able to meet people and get involved with cycling activities if you so choose. Every city

Cyclists are generally fun people to be around.

Bike riding will undoubtedly expose you to new places and people.

in the country has clubs, races, fun rides and tours, and a host of other bicycling related events. In addition, there are a lot of cycling vacations to both remote and populated locations. Backroads Tours, for example, has specific tours designed for families, couples, or singles. If you would like to meet new people, cycling is an excellent way to do it.

Conversely, biking can be done alone, without the interference of other people. Many cyclists use the sport to release the tensions of work and everyday life. If you are looking for a means to release built-up stress, look no further—nothing is better than going for a bike ride! Problems and worries literally melt away as you begin to log up the miles. You'll find that you can think more clearly after a bike ride and that solutions to your problems will present themselves. Riding a bike will improve your perspective and allow you to see things more clearly. It's hard to find solutions for problems when you are sitting indoors feeling depressed. Get outside and go for a bike ride!

Anyone can ride a bike, which makes it an ideal family activity. Wouldn't you like to find a sport your entire family, or group of friends, can enjoy together? Bike riding can be done by anyone, practically anywhere. It can be hard to come up with a group vacation that everyone will enjoy. Skiing and scuba diving, for example, require special skills and training. A cycling vacation, on the other hand, can be enjoyed by anyone at any age.

Riding a bike will make you sexy. Within a few weeks of riding, your body will begin to become more toned and you will start to drop excess weight. Whether you want to be or not, the new and improved you is going to be more physically attractive as a result of riding a bike. In addition, you'll feel better about yourself as you see and feel the changes and improvements taking place. The result will be increased self-confidence, which also will draw new people to you. Exercise improves circulation and muscle tone, oxygenates body tissue, and helps drop excess weight. You will be much more in tune with your physical self as a result, and you will be in better shape. You will also be able to enjoy other activities more as a result of the exercise obtained from bike riding.

Bike riding will open the door to new experiences. Most cyclists eventually take trips by bike. Traveling through new areas and cultures by bike is a lot of fun. Wouldn't you rather see the giant redwoods in northern California from a bike seat than from inside a car? Traveling by bike puts you in the fresh air where you can be a part of the experience, rather than being just an observer. You'll be more likely to stop and explore if you are traveling by bike than if you pass something at sixty miles an hour in a car.

You will even discover new experiences right where you live. There is probably a bikepath a few miles from where you are sitting right now, which you don't currently know anything about. Most bikepaths travel through scenic areas and are a relaxing way to spend a couple of hours.

Cycling is good for the environment. I wish everyone would leave their cars at home and commute by bike. Getting around by bike is a simple, easy, and effective way for you personally to do something to help clean up the environment, and that should make you feel good! The first time you come to a stop behind a bus or car, you'll get a firsthand example of how foul car exhaust is.

Cycling is a practical solution to improving air quality ... and it's fun.

THE HISTORY OF CYCLING

The concept of using bikes as a means of daily transportation isn't new. If you had been a postman in 1881, you might have made your rounds on a tricycle. You would have been very fashionable on your new bike and would probably have been drawn into debates about the latest developments in bike design and what was best. Historically speaking, the late 1800s were an exciting time for cycling enthusiasts since new designs of cycles were introduced almost yearly. In fact, the modern bicycle evolved in an amazingly short time from the Draisienne to the safety bicycle in less than seventy years!

The Hobby Horse

Introduced in 1817 by inventor Karl Drais, Freiherr Von Sauerbon, the *Draisienne* was an early two-wheeled "bike-like" vehicle. The Draisienne, which looked like a "wooden horse," featured two metal wheels connected by a piece of wood or metal upon which some type of saddle was attached. The rider moved forward by walking or running his feet along the ground. Unfortunately for the rider, the Draisienne's front wheel couldn't be turned, making directional control basically impossible.

The Draisienne quickly became popular, and soon variations on the design appeared. The *Hobby Horse*, a steerable variation, was introduced a year later and rapidly became fashionable in America and Europe. Within a short time, Hobby

This 1819 aquatint by H. Alken depicts "Johnson's Pedestrian Hobby Horse Riding School in London." (Courtesy of the Smithsonian Institution.)

The man in this photograph is believed to be W.H. Miller, of Columbus, Ohio, second president of the League of American Wheelmen. Uniforms such as these were commonly used by bicycle club members. (Courtesy of the Smithsonian Institution.)

16 *SPINNING: A GUIDE TO THE WORLD OF CYCLING*

This early group of safety cyclists uses a rail attachment to enjoy a smooth ride on a spur line of the Pittsburgh and Western Railroad between Cluffs Mills and McCrays, Pennsylvania, in the 1890s. (Courtesy of the Smithsonian Institution.)

An 1869 velocipede. (Courtesy of the Smithsonian Institution.)

Horses were a common sight on streets, in parks, and on pedestrian walkways.

One important drawback to the Hobby Horse was the fact that it lacked any brakes. With no way of stopping, it could be a real danger to both the person riding it and anyone or anything nearby. Naturally, it wasn't long before it was banned in some areas for reasons of safety.

The Hobby Horse went through a series of refinements during the next few decades. One of the most important developments was made in Scotland by a blacksmith named Kirkpatrick MacMillan when he built a Hobby Horse with a rear wheel drive system. Made up of a series of levers and pedals, this development was significant because it allowed the rider to move the "bike" forward without putting his feet on the ground.

Although MacMillan proved the validity of his machine by riding it seventy miles on one occasion, and a few copies of his design were made by other people, his design was never made popular. His contribution is historically significant because MacMillan's bike was the first to feature rear wheel drive—a feature that was to become standard forty years later.

The Velocipede

The *Velocipede*, also known as the "boneshaker" for its rough ride, was the first widely popular and accepted bicycle design. It featured pedals that were attached to the front wheel and also incorporated a crude brake, making it safer to ride than the Hobby Horse.

By the mid-1860s, Velocipedes were being manufactured in both America and Europe. They looked a lot like their Hobby Horse ancestor—basically two wheels attached by a beam—except pedals were attached to the front wheel and a cord ran from a lever next to the rear wheel to the handlebars. Braking was accomplished by pulling the cord.

The Velocipede became an established part of American culture during the 1860s. Riding schools were established to teach an eager public the fine art of bike riding.

Naturally, it wasn't long before competitive matches were organized. One of the earliest recorded races took place on May 31, 1868 in Paris on a 1,200 meter track, and was won by James Moore. The concept of bicycle racing caught on rapidly, since the races provided an ideal forum to test both design modifications and riding skills.

The High Bicycle

One of the primary pursuits of bicycle designers has always been speed. How do we make it go faster? In the late 1860s, the answer seemed simple. Make the front wheel as big as possible! Since the pedals were attached directly to the front wheel, increasing the size of the front wheel resulted in the bike rolling farther with every revolution of the pedals. As the front wheel became larger, the rear wheel was made smaller to help cut down on the bike's weight.

Referred to as an *Ordinary Bicycle*, a *Penny Farthing*, or a *High Bicycle*, this design concept resulted in some very unusual looking bikes. Some of the bikes of this design were also fairly dangerous and difficult to ride.

Replacing the Velocipede in the 1870s, and remaining popular until almost the end of the century, the High Bicycle saw rapid improvements in many aspects of its design.

A sidesaddle version was introduced for female riders. Various forms of suspension were created, such as saddles mounted on springs. The concept of radial spokes that could be adjusted by means of a nipple in the rim was introduced in the early 1870s. Hollow tubing, which cut down on weight, was also first used on high bicycles. The bike's tires were usually made of leather or solid rubber.

The High Bicycle remained at the peak of popularity throughout the 1880s. Racing became a favored spectator sport and drew large crowds on both sides of the Atlantic.

The bicycle transcended class differences and brought together people of different backgrounds. Clubs, such as The Cyclists Touring Club, were formed, and touring the countryside became a popular pastime.

Although the High Bicycle enjoyed tremendous success, it also had some major drawbacks. Most obvious was how high the rider rode above the ground. Falling off the bike could easily result in a serious injury.

Another problem was the fact that only strong individuals could power the big wheels on the bikes. Without any form of gearing, one had to turn the entire wheel with each rotation of the pedals. The larger the wheel, the greater the strength required.

The fact that the Penny Farthing required a riding technique that had to be taught was another drawback. A novice cyclist confronted with the High Bicycle had to wonder, "How do you get on and off?" Incidentally, riders mounted the High Bicycle by putting one foot on a mounting step while they pushed the bike along with the other. Once sufficient momentum had been gained, the rider "stepped" up and onto the saddle and began pedaling.

The Safety Bicycle

Towards the end of the 1800s, the *Safety Bicycle* began to be established as a safer, more efficient bicycle design. Although crude by modern standards, the safety bicycle was the basis for bicycle designs still in use today.

The bicycle was considered "safe" because the rider no longer rode high above the ground. The safety bicycle featured rear wheel drive by means of a chain, chain ring, and gears. Also, the Safety Bicycle wasn't limited to athletic individuals— it could be ridden and enjoyed by anyone.

The Rover was one of the first popular models to be widely manufactured. When George Smith rode a Rover on September 26, 1885 to set a new 100-mile record time of seven hours, five minutes, it became clear that the rear drive design was an improvement over the high wheel, front wheel drive bikes.

By the end of the century, pneumatic tires had become standard on most bikes. In addition to increasing the bike's efficiency while decreasing the amount of effort needed to pedal, pneumatic tires also greatly increased the rider's comfort by softening the bike's ride.

The modern bike had basically arrived. By the turn of the century, there were approximately 200 manufacturers producing over 3,000 different models.

2
The Bike

Fortunately for the modern-day cyclist, there have been a lot of improvements in cycling equipment since the safety bicycle of the late 1800s. Educating yourself about bikes and cycling equipment is important since using the right equipment can dramatically affect your enjoyment and performance of the sport.

CHOOSING THE RIGHT EQUIPMENT

For example, my friend Gail is in much better shape than I am. She goes to the gym almost every day and works out for hours doing aerobics; after the gym she goes running, bike riding, and swimming.

Considering how fit Gail is, it's easy to understand why I felt a little apprehensive the first time we went bike riding together. To increase the odds of being able to keep up with her on our thirty-mile ride, I suggested we take the flat bikepath along the coast.

The day of the ride came, and Gail met me at the beach with her bike. The first few miles we rode fairly slowly and warmed up as we passed through the Marina. Once past the harbor's congestion, the bikepath travels along the ocean uninterrupted for fifteen miles. With nothing obstructing our route, I began to pick up the pace. Naturally, it surprised me that Gail seemed to be having trouble keeping up. Twenty miles into the ride, I was having to consciously ride slowly to avoid leaving Gail behind. The last few miles, I rode at "normal" speed and finished almost ten minutes ahead of my friend.

Why was I able to ride so much faster than someone who was unquestionably in better shape than myself? EQUIPMENT! Gail was riding a mountain bike ... I was on a road bike. In addition to the mountain bike weighing more than my road bike, it also forced Gail to ride in an upright position—a major disadvantage when riding into the strong winds that blow off

This hybrid bike costs about $1,000 and is ideal for both paved and unpaved roads.

Many off-road bikes feature thumb shifters, such as this unit on my Mongoose.

Mountain bikes can be a good choice for inner city riding if you anticipate treating the bike roughly.

This tandem bike uses the Kinetic Seatpost to absorb shock. (Photo courtesy of Kinetic Concepts.)

the Pacific Ocean. The road bike put me in a bent over, wind-resistant position, making riding into the wind much easier. Another disadvantage for Gail was the gearing. Had we been traveling up extremely steep hills, the mountain bike's gearing would have excelled and left the road bike in the dust. The large knobby tires on Gail's mountain bike, which are designed for holding a line in dirt and mud, required a lot more pedaling effort than the thin slick tires of the road bike.

Now I'm not knocking mountain bikes; in fact, I have two of them and I love riding in the dirt! The point I'm trying to make is that it's important to buy the right type of bike, one that's matched to the kind of riding you are planning to do.

COST

There is an extremely wide price range to choose from when shopping for a bike. Good bikes can be bought for under $500 ... excellent bikes for $600 to $1,000 ... and top quality racing machines for up to $3,000. If you really want to get extreme, you can buy a custom bike for as much as $6,500 or more!

A lot of what "big" money buys in the bike market isn't worthwhile for the average rider. Why? Because what you're getting (generally) for the larger price is a lighter weight bike and better components. I ride a couple times a week on a $700 Mongoose mountain bike with a group of friends on a local trail. During the past year, some of our group has switched from $700 bikes to $2,500 bikes. While these people definitely had a more enjoyable riding experience, their performance and time didn't really improve at all. True, their new bikes were two pounds lighter (and had "pro" level components) than their old, less expensive bikes ... but so what? The riders in our group aren't professional athletes. We're not in the kind of shape where times are decided by tenths of a second. I found that losing a few pounds myself did more for my riding ability than any amount of money could buy. The point is to be honest with yourself about the shape you're in when selecting a price range. Why spend $1,000 more to get a bike that's a pound lighter if you could simply skip a few desserts and lose three pounds for free?

If money is no object, then get a high end bike. It's a bit like driving an expensive car. The top-of-the-line bikes are luxurious, are smooth handling, and have nicer components (more on components later). Keep in mind, however, that unlike an expensive car, *you* are the engine! Don't expect an expensive bike to make up for your being out of shape.

24 *SPINNING: A GUIDE TO THE WORLD OF CYCLING*

ANATOMY OF A BICYCLE

(A) ***Tires***. Most bikes use clincher-style tires that are held on by air pressure and have a separate inner tube. Road bikes use smooth "slick" tires, while off-road bikes use knobby tires. Tires cost between $20 and $100 and should be replaced at least once a year—more if you ride frequently.

(B) ***Rim***. Rims cost between $35 and $100 and will easily last many years if you don't crash or abuse them. It's important to get a rim that has the same number of spoke holes as your bike's hub. There are different style rims, each with its own matching style of tire, so be sure that your tires and rims are compatible when replacing one or the other.

(C) ***Spokes***. Spokes occasionally break or need adjusting. The cost of a single spoke is usually less than $2.50, so it's a good idea to keep a spare with you. Spokes generally will last a few years if you don't abuse them. When buying replacement spokes, be sure to get ones that are the same length as the ones on your wheel.

(D) ***Hub***. This Mongoose bike features quick release hubs, as do most quality bicycles. Hubs cost anywhere from $40 to several hundred dollars, so there's a wide range of choices out there. Be sure that the hub you buy has the same number of spoke holes as the rim you plan to match it with. Hubs can be overhauled and should basically last forever if you don't crash or abuse them. After a crash, you may need to replace the hub's axle if it is bent; a hub axle should cost about $15.

(E) *Fork*. There are many replacement forks available. A simple fork may cost $40, while a full suspension model such as Rock Shox's excellent suspension forks can cost close to $400. It's important to make sure the fork's steering tube is the same length as the bike's head tube, otherwise the fork's steering tube will need to be cut down. If you don't crash, your bike's fork will last forever.

(F) *Front Brake*. Naturally, there's also a rear brake, but it is not labeled in this photograph because it's basically identical to the front brake. Brakes can be overhauled and usually last several years, but *brake pads* may wear out in less than a year and will require replacing. Brake pads usually cost less than $20 a pair. *Brake cables* may also need replacing when they become rusted or look like there is a risk of them breaking ... usually every two years, depending upon how often you ride.

(G) *Brake Lever*. Generally, the brake lever and gear shifter on the left side of the bike control the front brake and derailleur, and the right side brake and gear shift levers control the rear brake and derailleur. Brake levers will usually last the life of the bike, but many cyclists replace their brake levers for lighter or more ergonomic models. The cost ranges from $20 to over $200. Often the type of material dictates the cost.

(H) *Grips*. Road bikes that feature down handlebars use grip tape, while rubber grips are used on bikes that feature upright handlebars. There's a wide variety of grip styles to choose from, with cost ranging from $5 to $30. Grips generally last a year or more, but you may end up cutting them off if you replace the bike's handlebars.

(I) *Stem*. Your bike's stem will basically last forever unless you have a bad crash, but some cyclists like to replace their stem with an extremely light model, or they replace it to obtain a more comfortable fit on the bike. Cost ranges from $40 to several hundred dollars. Titanium stems, for example, can get very expensive but are also extremely lightweight.

(J) *Headset*. The headset holds the fork in place. If the bike's steering becomes loose, you'll need to adjust the headset to eliminate the problem.

(K) *Top Tube*. It's easy to remember the name of this tube since it's on the top of the bike. Top tube length greatly influences a bike's fit, so it's important to have some idea of the size top tube you like, something that can only be established through experience. Generally, when you sit on the bike and hold the handlebars, the handlebars should block the front wheel's hub from view. If the hub can be seen in front of the handlebars, the top tube may be too short. If the hub can be seen behind the handlebars, the top tube may be too long. Stem length also has a bearing on how well a bike fits you.

(L) *Down Tube*. This is another part of the frame that dictates a bike's overall size.

(M) *Chain Rings*. Off-road bikes, such as this Mongoose, feature three chain rings. The smallest chain ring (also known as a "granny gear") is for steep uphill climbs. Road bikes usually only have two chain rings, although touring bikes often have three, since steep uphills may be encountered. Chain rings usually last a couple of years and cost $50 to several hundred dollars, depending upon the material.

(N) *Chain*. Chains may wear out at around 2,000 miles, some last much longer ... cost is usually less than $25.

(O) *Crankarms*. Crankarms, which the pedals are attached to, can also be replaced with lightweight (and expensive) material. Cost for lightweight chain rings and crankarms can get as high as $450.

(P) *Pedals*. Pedals last quite a few years. There are a few different styles to choose from, so you may decide to change whatever pedals come with your bike. If you know what you want in advance, it may be possible to negotiate the upgrade as part of the bike's purchase price. Toe clips are shown on this Mongoose, but clipless pedals would also be an option.

(Q) *Chainstay*. Part of the bike's frame, the chainstay's length is taken into consideration when determining a bike's overall size.

(R) *Saddle*. Since there are a lot of different models to choose from, replace your bike's saddle if it is uncomfortable. Cost ranges from $30 to over $100, with lightweight materials being used in the upper price range.

(S) *Rear Derailleur*. If you damage the bike's derailleur in a crash, it may need to be replaced. Cost ranges from $30 to $150. Derailleurs will usually last quite a few years if not abused. Keeping them clean can go a long way towards extending their life.

(T) *Seatstay*. Part of the bike's frame, its length has an effect on a bike's overall size.

(U) *Seatpost*. This is another bike part that is frequently replaced with a lightweight part. Cost ranges from $20 to well over $100 for a titanium piece. Make sure you get a seatpost that is long enough.

(V) *Seat Tube*. The length of the seat tube is one of the primary measurements used to determined the size of the bike's frame. It is important to know what size seat tube you like, something that can only be determined through experience. There are a few different mathematical equations that use your inseam length to determine what size frame is right for you. However, people's bodies often don't fit standard formulas, so the best way to determine size is to get on the bike and ride. Custom frames allow you to get a frame built exactly to your body's specifications.

(W) *Rear Dropout*. Both the front and rear wheels on this Mongoose mountain bike feature quick release hubs that allow the wheels to "dropout" from the frame easily. The quick release mechanisms can be replaced with lightweight models; cost varies depending upon the material.

(X) *Front Derailleur*. Replacing the front derailleur after a crash may cost between $20 and $100. The front derailleur will usually last for the life of the bike if it's not abused.

(Y) *Bottom Bracket*. You can't really see the bottom bracket in this picture since it is inside the frame. The bottom bracket contains the spindle, which is the axle that connects the two crankarms. Your bike's bottom bracket may need replacing after a year ... or it may last for the lifetime of the bike. Cost is in the $30 to $150 range, depending on the model and the material used. The bottom bracket is one item that sometimes breaks early in a bike's life ... and sometimes doesn't.

(Z) *Head Tube*. The head tube houses the fork's steering tube and is part of the bike's frame. If you are replacing the fork, it's important to know the length of your head tube. You will want to make sure the new fork's steering tube is the same length.

TYPES OF BIKES

Bicycles can be broken into six basic groups. Before you buy a bike, give some thought as to where you will be riding it, how far you will be riding, and how often you will be riding. Also, try to rent a few different types of bikes before you buy. You may find, for instance, that you don't like a certain type of shift lever or handlebar design. Following are descriptions of the six basic types of cycles available today.

Coaster Brakes

Coaster brakes is the term used to describe the category of "gearless" bikes that are common along boardwalks and other low mileage/easy terrain environments. These bikes only have one gear on the back wheel and don't have any type of gear shifting. Braking is accomplished by pedaling backwards. Probably the first bike you owned as a child was some type of coaster brake model.

Beach Cruisers

Beach cruisers are set up for comfortable "cruising" along easy terrain. They're basically an adult version of a kid's bike and are a lot of fun to rent. Beach cruisers are common sights in bike rental departments, at beaches, and at parks since their simple design means they are easy to maintain and hard to damage.

Beach cruisers feature wide padded seats, high handlebars, and wide stable tires. While most feature coaster brakes, some do have a few gears and hand brakes. I wouldn't buy a beach cruiser with gears. If you want gears, you would be better off moving up to one of the other categories of bikes.

The advantage of a beach cruiser is that they are cheap to buy (around $100) and easy to ride. If you are not planning to ride very far or very often, then a bike of this type may be ideal for you.

The disadvantage to beach cruisers is that they are not suitable for much other than flat terrain and short distances. If you want to ride fast or up steep hills, you will most likely find a beach cruiser too limiting. They are fun, however, for just cruising along the bikepath at ten miles an hour.

Mountain Bikes

Mountain bikes have been enjoying great popularity in the last few years. Designed for "off-road" use, mountain bikes evolved from BMX Stunt Bikes in the late 1970s. BMX bikes are designed primarily for high stunt jumping (and crashing) and usually don't have any gears or other "breakable" equipment. Mountain bikes, on the other hand, offer a full selection of gears and other high-tech equipment.

Mountain bikes are truly designed to be ridden off-road. They feature wide "knobby" tires for traction, straight handlebars for control over a wide variety of terrains, and gearing suitable for going up and down steep hills. Most manufacturers offer at least one model with front suspension, and some offer both front and rear suspension. Almost all mountain bikes have triple chain rings to tackle steep mountains with relative ease!

Components on mountain bikes are heavier and more rugged than what is found on road bikes. These bikes can take the abuse (if you can) of blasting down a rut-filled hillside at high speed. Try that with a road bike and you will most likely end up with a set of bent rims.

If you think you'll be riding primarily off-road, then a mountain bike is the best choice for you. Would you like to spend a weekend camping away from civilization in the wilderness? A mountain bike will get you and your equipment there and back.

Factory built mountain bikes can cost anywhere from $250 to $3,000. You can buy an excellent bike for about $700. Custom-built mountain bikes can generally be had for between $2,500 and $6,000.

Road Bikes

Road bikes, as their name implies, are designed to be used on paved surfaces. They are much more aerodynamic than mountain bikes and feature "drop" handlebars, thin tires, and a wide range of gears. Road bikes are considerably less rugged than mountain bikes. Treat a road bike as roughly as you would a mountain bike and you will destroy it.

Road bikes are much faster and easier to ride than mountain bikes (providing you're not on a mountain). The thin tires found on most road bikes roll with much less resistance than the knobby tires common on most mountain bikes. If you plan to ride on paved surfaces most of the time—for fairly long distances—

then this is the type of bike for you. I say long distances because if you are only going to ride a few miles at a time, then any bike will do.

Racing bikes are road bikes that have been set up to be as light as possible. They also feature components that are conducive to road racing. Although racing bikes look identical to common road bikes, they are generally not as rugged. However, since these bikes have been designed to win road races, it's fun to ride them on the road even if you're not a racer. The line between road bikes and true racing bikes is often a little blurry. Basically, if you are on a road bike that costs more than a $1,000, it's a racing bike. If you can afford it and plan on only riding on well-maintained paved surfaces, try a racing bike!

Touring bikes are road bikes that have been set up for long distance touring. Touring bikes are heavier than non-touring road bikes because they are designed to be strong, durable, and capable of carrying heavy loads in saddlebags and other accessories. They also feature fairly wide tires (by road bike standards) for better traction, and a "granny gear" (a small third chain ring) for steep hill climbs. If you think you may eventually get into touring, a touring bike may be for you.

Road bikes in their various configurations will cost anywhere between $200 and $6,500.

Hybrid Bikes

Hybrid bikes, also called *cross-trainer bikes*, are a cross between road bikes and mountain bikes. They feature knobby tires that are wider than what is found on the average road bike, but are not as heavy and wide as mountain bike tires. With a hybrid bike, you can jump off a high street curb—something you shouldn't do with a road bike's delicate rims and tires. Hybrid bikes aren't, however, as tough and heavy as mountain bikes.

Hybrid bikes come in a variety of configurations. They offer you a choice between drop handlebars and upright bars, and also can be had with either semi-knobby or slick tires. How you outfit the bike depends on its intended use.

I like hybrid bikes. They are great for riding along the well-maintained dirt roads in Vermont. They're also ideal for riding in the city where you may encounter potholes that would eat a true road bike. While I enjoy riding my road bike at a high speed on bikepaths and uncrowded highways, I much prefer riding my Mongoose hybrid within the city. If I hit, or hop off, a curb, it's not a big deal. Not wanting to thrash my road bike or ride my heavy mountain bike, the hybrid bike fills the gap perfectly.

Tandem Bikes and Others

Tandem bikes are designed to carry two people. Tandem bikes come in both road and off-road configurations and generally cost between $1,000 and $3,000.

In addition to tandems, there are other types of bikes, but they are not that common. *Tricycles*, for example, have been making a comeback along flat bikepaths, in rental departments, at parks, and at beaches.

Recumbent cycles, on which the rider sits in a small "chair" with the pedals in front of him, are another variation that is occasionally seen.

WHAT BIKE SHOULD YOU BUY?

Basically, you should buy a bike that fits you well and is designed for the type of riding you plan to do. It's also a good idea to buy your bike from a reputable store where you will be assured of service should a problem develop.

My favorite bike is made by Mongoose. The reasons I use Mongoose bikes can also be applied to whatever brand you might be considering.

Fit

As stated previously, fit and comfort are the most important features to seek initially when shopping for a bike. Some brands come in a few generic sizes, making it hard to find a model that fits you well. Mongoose, for my body size, is one of the only brands that makes frames I find comfortable.

Components

Mongoose bikes come in enough different component packages to fit every budget. What's nice is that the same frame is used on many of their models, so you can upgrade your bike at a later date if you wish. My bikes take quite a beating while my friends and I test out different ideas ... and we've yet to destroy a Mongoose bike. Some other brands we have used in the past have literally cracked after a few months of use.

After-Market Compatibility

There are so many products available as after-market accessories that it is important to own a bike that uses standard sizes so you can customize if you want to. For example, you don't want to discover that you can't add a particular brand of front suspension forks because your bike's steering tube is a weird diameter.

It's helpful to become familiar with the various parts of a bike before you buy. It may be possible to exchange a particular item for something that is more suitable to your needs. A good place to start is the bike's saddle.

SADDLES

"My legs feel great ... but my butt is killing me!" is a common statement from many people after their first hour or two on a bike. In fact, a sore butt has probably driven more novices out of cycling than anything else! Ironically, it's easy to avoid. You have to ride fairly often (at least twice a week) and use the correct type of saddle for the type of riding you do. Although most people don't believe it, the small, hard bike seats are often the most comfortable if you plan to ride frequently.

While most bikes come with decent saddles, you may choose to purchase an after-market seat to meet your comfort needs. Some features you should consider include:

Gel Seats

Gel seats, as their name implies, have a gel-based substance that offers padding between your butt and the seat. The gel is non-compressible, and therefore doesn't "flatten out" after a lot of use. It does, however, slightly conform to your anatomical shape while you ride. One thing to keep in mind is that less expensive gel saddles sometimes use a gel that can harden with age. Expect to pay between $25 and $50 for a gel saddle.

Racing Saddles

Racing saddles are usually extremely narrow and are designed to be light. The narrow saddles eliminate any possibility of chafing during long rides. If you are primarily a recreational rider, these saddles may not be for you, since you need to ride a few times a week to avoid soreness. However, if you log 100 or more miles a week and ride at least three times a week, you may want to consider purchasing a racing saddle. Naturally, racers prefer these saddles. Expect to pay between $50 and $80.

Recently, some manufacturers have come out with racing saddles that feature titanium frames and rails. The advantage is a lightweight saddle ... at a price of about $100. Some friends of mine swear by these seats and tell me that they are the most comfortable around.

Leather Saddles

Leather saddles are preferred by some riders because they can be broken in through use to conform to a rider's contours, making them extremely comfortable. Some models feature a bolt under the front of the seat that allows the user to tighten the leather as it stretches. Brooks, the most popular manufacturer of leather saddles, makes a "pre-softened" leather seat that requires very little break-in. One disadvantage to leather saddles is they do not respond well if left in the rain. Expect to pay around $100 for a leather saddle.

Foam Saddles

Foam padded seats are less expensive than most other saddles and may be a good choice for recreational riders who do not ride very often. These seats have a layer of foam padding to help alleviate saddle soreness. Most are priced in the $30 range.

Liquid Saddles

The term "liquid" is a little misleading. These saddles feature a soft, gel-like substance that conforms to a rider's shape. The liquid is softer than the gel found in gel saddles. These seats have been compared to ski boots that feature foam-filled bladders conforming to a skier's foot. Some seats of this type have price tags of about $200.

Anatomical Saddles

Some manufacturers offer seats that recognize that men and women are anatomically different. Women riders may wish to look into some of the options available. Prices are in the $40 range.

SHIFTING SYSTEMS

There is a bewildering selection of shifting systems available to cyclists today. Which one you choose is a personal decision based on your body type and the type of riding you do. So what shifting system is right for you? The only way to really tell is to rent or borrow a bike that features the system you plan to buy in order to try it out first. Some of the more popular ones include:

Down-Tube Levers

These are the traditional shift levers most people are familiar with. Their name comes from the fact that they are located on the "down-tube" of the bicycle's frame. Learning to shift takes a little practice since you must remove one hand from the handlebars and reach down to the shift levers. Generally, down-tube levers are found on most inexpensive road bikes (and some high-priced ones, too).

Thumb Shifters

Thumb shifters were the "standard" on mountain bikes for a long time. This has changed, however, with all the new shifting systems on the market. Thumb shifters sit on the handlebars and offer the convenience of being able to shift without changing your hand position. Thumb shifters can be mounted on top of or below the handlebars.

Grip Shifters

As their name implies, grip shifters are a part of the bike's handlebar grips. Mountain bike versions allow you to shift without changing your hand position since the shifter actually replaces the bike's grips completely. To change gears, you simply twist the end of the grip.

Road bike grip shifters are usually an extension of the handlebars and still require you to move your hand to change gears. Cost ranges from $70 to $100.

Sachs Power Grip and Twist Ring

Here is a method of shifting that is really terrific on upright handlebars because it allows you to shift without moving your hand position at all. The Power Grip allows you to make gear changes by twisting the handlebar grip. This arrangement is great when riding over rough terrain because it lets the rider keep both hands firmly on the grips, maintaining control. The Power Grip features a lock button to prevent unintentional gear shifts. For information about the Sachs Power Grip and Twist Ring, contact:

Sachs Bicycle Components
22445 East La Palma Avenue
Yorba Linda, CA 92686
(714) 692-6696

Incidentally, Sachs is one of the leading distributors of bicycle chains and their prices are very reasonable.

Bar-Ends Shift Levers

These mount at the end of the handlebars and are easier to reach than down-tube levers. Bar-end shifters are generally only used on drop handle bars.

Campagnolo Ergopower™

This system features a small lever just to the inside of the brake levers and is operated with your thumb. It's a nice setup because you don't need to remove your hands from the brake levers while shifting. Cost is in the $400 range.

Shimano Dual Control™

This is another system that is ideal for road bikes, since you don't need to change your hand position at all to shift gears. Shifting is accomplished by moving the brake levers. Bikes that feature this system generally cost well over $1,000.

BRAKES

There was a time when riding a bike with brakes was considered unmanly, which caused many foolhardy individuals to remove the brakes from their bikes to prove they were fearless. Stopping was accomplished by hopping off, sliding into the ground, or hitting a solid object. Thankfully, those days have passed and now even we manly men ride with brakes.

All the braking systems found on name-brand bikes work well. Most road bikes use either *side pull* or *center pull* brakes, while mountain and hybrid bikes generally use *cantilever brakes*. Center or side pull brakes feature brake arms, with the cable attaching on top or on the side of the brake. Cantilever brakes don't have brake arms and are connected by the cable, which forms a "Y".

Some bikes use a *disc brake*. Tandem bikes, for example, with the weight of two riders, can gain a lot of momentum ... especially while going down a steep, rutted dirt hill. Some tandem riders feel that stopping within a safe distance is made easier with a disc brake (although many tandem bikes don't use them).

PEDALS

Bicycle pedals come in three configurations. The basic pedal, which comes on most beach cruisers, coaster brake models, BMX, and kids' bikes, doesn't provide any way to attach your foot to the pedal. These types of pedals are fine for occasional recreational use, but they aren't very efficient. They are ideal for children since you don't want a young child's foot bound to the bike.

Toe Clips

Toe clips are basically small baskets for your toes, which hold your feet on the pedals. This arrangement allows you to pedal with greater efficiency. Some toe clips are after-market add-ons; others are actually built into the pedal.

One advantage to toe clips is that you can use non-cycling shoes with them. For example, I often loan my "second" bike to friends who want to ride with me just for a day. For this reason, I leave the toe clips on that bike so it can be used by anyone regardless of what type of shoe the person is wearing.

A disadvantage to toe clips is that they are a little awkward to use, especially when you first start pedaling and are getting your feet into the toe clips. It's possible to lose a couple of seconds "fumbling" with your toe clips, which is a real disadvantage in a race.

Toe clips can be bought for as little as $20. Low cost is an advantage of toe clips.

Clipless Pedals

Clipless pedals are used by most serious cyclists. These pedals attach to a cleat on the bottom of your shoe. Clipless pedals must be used in conjunction with a matching cleat and

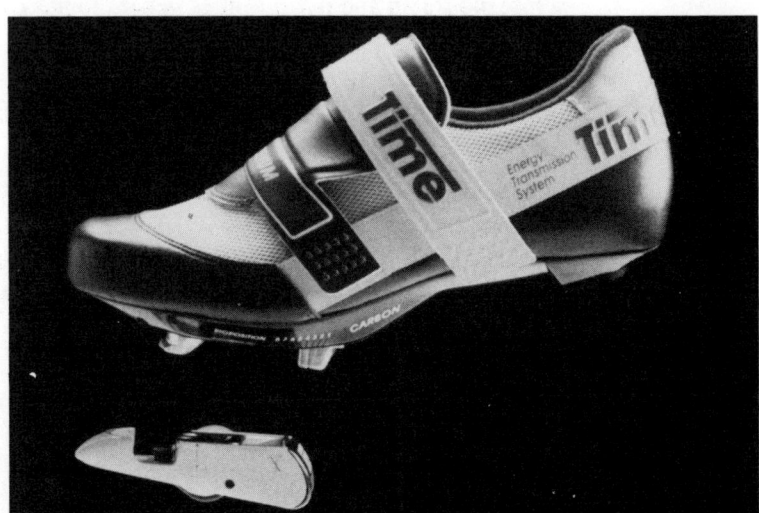

COLOR SLIDE 6. Most serious cyclists use a clipless pedal and matching shoe. (Photo courtesy of Time.)

shoe, which is also their one disadvantage.

Clipless pedals are easy to use; you simply "snap" into the cleat and start pedaling. On most models, you release your foot by twisting your heel outward. Your foot is also released during a fall (similar to a ski binding) when excess pressure is exerted on your foot. Cost for a clipless pedal system with shoes ranges from $100 to over $300.

TIRES

The type of tire you put on your bike can greatly affect its performance. When you buy a bike, chances are, the tires it comes with are well suited for the type of riding the manufacturer expected the bike to be used for. You may, however, need to change the tires to meet your specific needs.

Hybrid bikes, for example, often come with semi-knobby tires that aren't really suited to hard pavement. They are also not suited to off-road riding in the dirt. If you are planning to use the bike primarily, or exclusively, on paved roads, you should probably switch to a "slick" road tire to cut down on rolling resistance. Matching the correct tire to the type of riding you do can dramatically improve your bike's performance.

It is possible to put slick road tires on a mountain bike. The heavy knobby tires that most mountain bikes come with are ideal for blasting down dirt hills. However, most people seem to use their mountain bikes primarily on paved surfaces. Switching to a road tire will make these bikes much easier to pedal.

3
Accessories & Custom Equipment

There are many accessories available to enhance your cycling enjoyment. One of the most useful is a cycling computer, which mounts on your bike's handlebars and supply you with a variety of useful information. They are lightweight and easy to use—I recommend you get one! A basic model might feature a speedometer, an odometer, and an elapsed time indicator. Cost for the simpler computers can be as low as $25.

COMPUTERS

An advanced computer ($40 to $100) will offer more sophisticated versions of all the above items, and may also display cadence, distance to destination, and a variety of other information.

I've been using Avenir computers. I like them because they are extremely durable (some of the other brands I've used have died after crashing), are easy to install, and offer a lot of features. For information about Avenir cycling computers, contact:

Avenir
4030 Via Pescador
Camarillo, CA 93012-9864

Before purchasing a computer, it's helpful to become familiar with the features available. Following are some of the more common features offered.

Speedometer

The speedometer displays your current speed and is useful when you want to maintain a constant speed. For example, say you want to go for a thirty-mile ride, but have to be back in two hours due to a commitment later in the day. Referring to your bike's speedometer and never dropping below fifteen miles an hour would ensure the desired timetable.

Cycling computers are easy to learn to use.

Odometer

The odometer displays the total mileage acquired from the moment the computer is put on the bike. Most cyclists feel a sense of accomplishment when they hit landmark distances, such as watching the odometer register 1,000. Some of the less expensive computers' odometers are erased if you remove the battery or if the battery goes dead.

Distance Traveled

This is a trip odometer that you can reset to zero anytime you like. At the beginning of every ride, for example, you can set it to zero to keep track of the day's mileage.

On some inexpensive computers, setting the distance traveled to zero resets everything to zero (except the odometer). This can be annoying if, for example, you don't want to stop the timer but do want to set the mileage to zero. What often separates the less expensive computers from the more expensive models is versatility within the features. A $50 computer may do basically the same thing as a $25 model, but it's going to do it better and with more versatility.

Timers and Clocks

There are lots of variations here. Some computers have a basic timer that you set to zero and then hit start. Others are capable of displaying total trip time and time of day and also have a separate stopwatch (useful for timing sprints, etc.).

Average Speed

The average speed display indicates the average speed of your ride. Some less expensive computers keep calculating when you stop riding (unless you turn them off). For example, my friend Tom and I recently compared average speeds at the end of a ride. Since we had ridden at basically the same speed throughout the ride, it was surprising to see his average speed was eight mph, while mine was fifteen mph. The reason? When we stopped for a cappuccino during the ride, Tom's computer had continued to calculate while his bike wasn't moving; mine had automatically stopped calculating during our "down time."

Maximum Speed

This function displays the maximum speed reached during the ride. Blasting down a hill at high speed can require full concentration, and you may choose to look at the road rather than at your computer. But not to worry. The maximum speed indicator will record the highest speed reached for later scrutiny. (My friend Tom hates it when I delete his highest speed before he gets a chance to show everyone.)

Cadence

The cadence display tells you how fast you are "spinning" —your r.p.m., in other words. Knowing your cadence is useful since your goal is to maintain a constant pace while you ride. As you start up a hill, the idea is to shift to an easier gear so that you can maintain the same cadence. This becomes very important if you want to improve aerobic fitness.

Altimeter

This feature tells you how much elevation you gain (or lose) during a ride. I've found that becoming familiar with elevation as it relates to distance is useful. If, for example, you are told that the course you plan to ride has an elevation gain of 600 feet over a steady four-mile stretch, it may be hard to visualize what that means. Riding with an altimeter on your training rides gives you the information necessary to become familiar with various altitude gains over a variety of distances. Incidentally, you may occasionally hear riders discuss a hill's elevation in percentages; for example, a six percent grade or an eight percent grade. This means you gain that many feet of elevation for every 100 feet of forward travel. For example, on a six percent grade, you'll gain six feet in elevation for every 100 feet of forward travel.

Knowing what these grades "feel like" to ride is useful. If you are on a tour and the leader tells you the day's ride includes a four-mile hill with an eight percent grade, you'll know what that means in terms of physical effort.

CLOTHING

Wearing clothes specifically designed for cycling will make you a lot more comfortable on the bike. While everyday sport clothes are adequate for an afternoon ride on a rental bike, they will become uncomfortable if you start riding regularly.

Shorts

If you only buy one item of bike clothing to start, get a pair of cycling shorts. Most are made of Lycra and fit snugly so that they don't bunch up the way other shorts will when you are riding. Cycling shorts also offer protection from chafing.

Cycling shorts have a built-in "pad" that puts a little cushion between your butt and the bike's seat. Most novice riders come to appreciate their first pair of cycling shorts for this reason alone.

Another reason you should wear cycling shorts is that they allow sweat to evaporate through the material. Cotton shorts (and shirts) become wet from sweat, which is uncomfortable, in addition to being potentially unhealthy and possibly causing skin rashes. Cycling shorts allow the moisture to escape.

Finally, cycling shorts are aerodynamic. In fact, you will probably feel faster as soon as you put on a pair!

Cycling shorts cost between $20 and $100.

Jerseys

Cycling shirts are called jerseys and are also made of Lycra. As with the shorts, they are aerodynamic, comfortable, and lightweight, and they allow moisture to escape.

Cycling jerseys usually have two or three pockets on the lower back. The pockets are located behind you to keep an aerodynamic profile. They are an ideal place to keep money, maps, snacks, extra water, and any other items you may want access to while riding.

Shoes

Cycling shoes have stiffer soles than normal shoes, which means you can transfer power to the bike's pedals more efficiently. The type of shoe you get will be determined by what type of cycling you do (mountain versus road), and whether or not you use clipless pedals.

Mountain biking shoes are often a little "beefier" than road biking shoes. Some shoes are designed to be used as walking shoes (sort of) in addition to cycling shoes. Others are pretty uncomfortable to walk in for any distance.

Most road riding shoes are lightweight. Racing shoes tend to be extremely lightweight and feature thin (but stiff) soles. I find the really thin soles uncomfortable since I begin to "feel" the pedals through the soles after a few miles. Many shoes do offer thick (and lightweight) soles, so you may want to keep this in mind when selecting a pair.

If you have clipless pedals on your bike, you will have to buy shoes that are compatible. Some systems have the cleat in the sole of the shoe, which is comfortable to walk in. Other shoes have the cleat sticking out past the sole, which is fairly uncomfortable (and noisy) to walk in.

It's possible to buy cycling shoes that can have cleats added later. This is ideal if you are now riding with toe clips but think you might buy clipless pedals sometime in the future.

Always wear socks when you ride to avoid blisters and absorb sweat. Most cyclists opt for thin, low-cut socks.

Gloves

Cycling gloves protect your hands during a fall. Imagine falling off your bike at twenty miles an hour. What will you do to help break your fall? Probably hold your hands out in front of you (although it is generally better to hang onto the handlebars and "ride" the bike down). Cycling gloves have padded palms that will help keep the skin on your hands during a fall.

Biking gloves also provide padding between your hands and the handlebars. If you ride a lot, it is possible to get blisters on your hands from friction on the handlebars. Buying a pair of padded gloves solves the problem.

Gloves also help you maintain a secure grip on the bars. As you ride, your hands may become sweaty, which can increase the chances of your grip slipping. Gloves basically eliminate this problem.

Rain Gear

Rain gear consists of waterproof pants and a jacket. Naturally, rain gear is also lightweight. If you are going on a multi-day tour, it may be prudent to bring along a set. Riding a bike soaking wet isn't much fun. Another option is not to ride in the rain.

44 SPINNING: A GUIDE TO THE WORLD OF CYCLING

Jay prefers to use a foot pump with his Mongoose IBOC mountain bike.

14. Always carry a portable pump on your bike.

If you only go on day rides, you probably don't need to buy rain gear—you can just ride on dry days. If you are planning to ride across one of the states, however, you'll need it.

WATER BOTTLES

You *must* drink water while you ride. A good rule of thumb is to drink *at least one bottle of water an hour* to avoid dehydration. When you buy your bike, get some water bottles and water bottle "cages" (which hold the bottles to your bike). Water bottles cost $1 to $6; cages from $2 to $15. It's money well spent.

TIRE PUMPS

Bicycle tires need to be pumped up every so often. With a road bike, you will lose speed as your tires become low on air since "soft" tires don't roll as efficiently as ones that are fully inflated. With a mountain bike, you may want to let air out of your tires when riding off-road, and then fully inflate them for riding on hard surfaces.

All tires have their working pressure stated on them in psi (pounds per square inch), such as 90 psi. Road tires generally operate at a higher psi than off-road tires. Unless you never plan on repairing a flat tire at the side of the road, you should buy a small portable pump to carry on your bike. It's important to match the pump with your tires' stem ... and to make sure it can be carried on your bike. Some pumps have reversible nozzles that can be used on more than one stem size. The best thing to do is buy the pump when you purchase your bike. Portable pumps cost between $15 and $50.

Most road bikes carry the pump underneath the top tube. On a mountain bike, the pump is often clamped on near the water bottle cage since there's a greater chance of the pump being knocked off in the road bike position.

You may also want to get a larger, easier-to-use pump and keep it in your garage or car. The larger pumps aren't bike portable, but they pump much faster and offer features such as easy-to-read pressure gauges. Cost ranges between $20 and $80.

LIGHTWEIGHT PARTS

There are lot of after-market lightweight replacement parts made for bicycles. Stems, handlebars, seatposts, rims, hubs, and just about any other part of your bike can be replaced with a lightweight piece. Rims are a good place to start if your bike came with heavy ones. If you are interested, take a look at the rims made by:

Weinmann Sports, Inc.
3 Union Drive
Olney, IL 62450
(800) 447-4588

Weinmann rims are extremely light and durable. Putting a Hyperlite Handlebar on your bike (made by Answer Products) is another good way to lighten your bike. Contact:

Answer Products
27460 Scott Avenue
Valencia, CA 91355
(805) 257-4411
FAX: (805) 257-4011

HEART MONITORS

A heart monitor is a useful training aid. There are two styles in use; one uses photo-electric sensors, the other uses electrodes usually placed on the chest or fingers. Heart monitors that use electrodes are more accurate and are what you should use. Cost is between $100 and $450.

A heart monitor is a good tool to use to gauge your fitness. For example, you can check your monitor to know your heart rate during exercise. Another gauge of how fit you are is how long it takes your pulse to recover after exercising.

One of the biggest advantages of a heart monitor is that it helps you avoid over-training. For example, if your pulse is higher than usual the morning after a ride, that may be an indication you are training too hard.

ROLLERS AND STATIONARY TRAINERS

If you want to be able to continue your training on days when conditions make it unsafe to ride, you might want to get a *stationary trainer*. Stationary trainers allow you to continue to train indoors so you don't lose conditioning when you can't get outside.

Stationary trainers also have the advantage of letting you ride when you are pressed for time. Many cyclists fit their "rides" in while watching the morning news before going to work. The concept is that any type of riding is better than no riding.

Rollers are a type of stationary trainer that don't support the bike. You ride the bike on the rollers, which turn under the bike's wheels. Rollers require you to keep your balance and they take a little practice to get used to. Track racers often use rollers to keep from cooling down between races.

Many cyclists prefer using a stationary trainer that either attaches to the front or back wheel of the bike. Most involve removing the front wheel and clamping the bike into a rack-like device while the back wheel rides on rollers.

One option you should consider is some type of fan to help keep you cool while you ride indoors. Riding indoors without a fan usually results in a puddle of sweat forming below the bike. A fan helps remove sweat, in addition to keeping you cool.

LOCKS

According to a recent bicycle magazine survey, over two million Americans had a bicycle stolen during the last three years! On many of the larger college campuses, an average of six to twelve bikes is stolen each week, and yearly losses often exceed $50,000. Clearly, you need a quality bicycle lock.

Ironically, many of the bikes stolen are locked ... but with poorly made locks. Make sure you purchase a good quality

Buy a good quality lock for your bike.
(Photo courtesy of Bad Bones.)

lock, such as the Bad Bones locks made by Integrated Cycle Systems (415) 543-4466, which is both strong and designed specifically to guard against being pried open.

I would suggest staying away from the cable and padlock combination-type locks. The cable adds unwanted weight when riding, as does the usually heavy padlock, and it is easily cut with a hacksaw or other cable-cutting device. Buy a lock specifically designed for bicycle security.

LIGHTS

Bicycle lights increase your vision in addition to making you more visible on the road. Having a light on your bike can also extend your riding time since you have the visibility to ride at dusk and after dark.

If you are planning on riding in traffic after dark, you will need both a headlight and a taillight. You should also consider getting one of the strobe lights that are made specifically for cyclists. Putting a strobe light on your leg increases your visibility since the light is then moving and blinking.

Putting a light on your bike will improve your visibility. (Photo courtesy of Todson.)

There are a lot of models available, ranging from complicated systems to small portable lights that can be clamped on and off your bike or body easily. Some features you should consider when buying a light are:

ACCESSORIES AND CUSTOM EQUIPMENT 49

Mounting

How difficult is it to mount the light on your bike? Some systems involve complicated clamps and wiring that are difficult and time-consuming to assemble. Consider whether or not you will be removing the light from your bike frequently. If the light is not a permanent fixture, then one of the smaller portable lights may be what you want.

Weight

How much does the light weigh? There are still some inexpensive designs out there. These use heavy batteries that will add considerable weight to your bike. Fortunately, there are also some excellent lightweight models to choose from. Shopping at a cycling specialty shop will help ensure a good selection.

Water Resistance

The last thing you want is for your light to go out when it's raining, leaving you to skid around cars in the darkness. Some lights are so waterproof they can actually be submerged in water. Other models start hovering on the edge of failure after getting splashed. Often, the bargain basement, super cheap lights are the ones that will fail early.

Ruggedness

The bicycle light will undergo a lot of jarring on the road. Make sure the light is built strongly enough to handle road shock and perhaps an occasional crash.

Lights can cost anywhere from $10 to over $200.

ROCK SHOX SUSPENSION

Blasting down a rock-covered road or hillside can be very tiring. Every bump and rut transmits shocks through the bike to your arms and legs, which act as shock absorbers. As you become tired, your arms stiffen and the ride becomes even more tiring.

One excellent solution is to put a pair of Rock Shox front suspension forks on your bike. Similar to a motorcycle's suspension system, the Rock Shox forks compress and absorb bumps in the road so your arms don't have to. They also feature a six-position adjustable setting, which allows you to dial in the amount of pressure needed before the fork will compress. For example, you may want a heavier setting for high speed downhills than you want on a slow ride on a relatively bump-free dirt road.

Front suspension gives you more control over the bike on rough terrain. Without the Rock Shox forks, the bike tends to get knocked off course. Front suspension minimizes this effect by absorbing the shock rather than letting it throw the front end of your bike to the side. For information about Rock Shox products, contact:

Rock Shox
2585 Leghorn Street
Mountain View, CA 94043
(800) 677-7177
(415) 967-SHOX
FAX: (415) 967-7487

PROTECTIVE GEAR

Off-road riding requires far more protective gear than road riding. In addition to a helmet, consider a pair of long-fingered motorcross gloves, shin protectors, knee pads, elbow pads, and wraparound goggles.

Protective gear does two things for you. Most important, it helps prevent injury during a fall. It also protects you from branches, other bikes, and anything else that could potentially whack you as you ride by.

Confidence is the second advantage of protective gear. Without protective gear, you may be scared of getting hurt—which can affect how you ride. The clothing normally worn by cyclists is lightweight and will provide zero protection should you find yourself hitting the gravel at twenty miles an hour.

BIKE RACKS AND BOXES

While it is possible simply to toss your bike in the backseat of your car, there are far superior methods of transporting your bike. To avoid damaging your bike, it is a good idea to use one of the specially designed bike racks that allow you to transport your bike—or many bikes—without damage.

The time may also come when you will want to ship your bike somewhere, perhaps for a bike tour or race. There are a few products available to make this chore easier, or you may choose simply to have a local bike shop box up your bike.

The *GTI Box and bike case* is an excellent product that can

ACCESSORIES AND CUSTOM EQUIPMENT   **51**

This rack made by Bike Tight is ideal if you have a truck or large car ... and there's even room for your cat.

Throwing your bike into the back of your car is the least desirable way to transport it.

be used to ship your bike or transport it strapped to your car. The case is capable of holding a complete bicycle—partially disassembled—with a frame of up to twenty-four inches. The box can also be used to carry other cargo when not used as a bike case.

The GTI Box measures less than 130 inches in length and girth combined and is made of rotomolded polyethylene, which is the same material used to make kayaks and is extremely strong.

The GTI box is big enough to carry a complete bike along with some additional cargo. (Photo courtesy of GTI.)

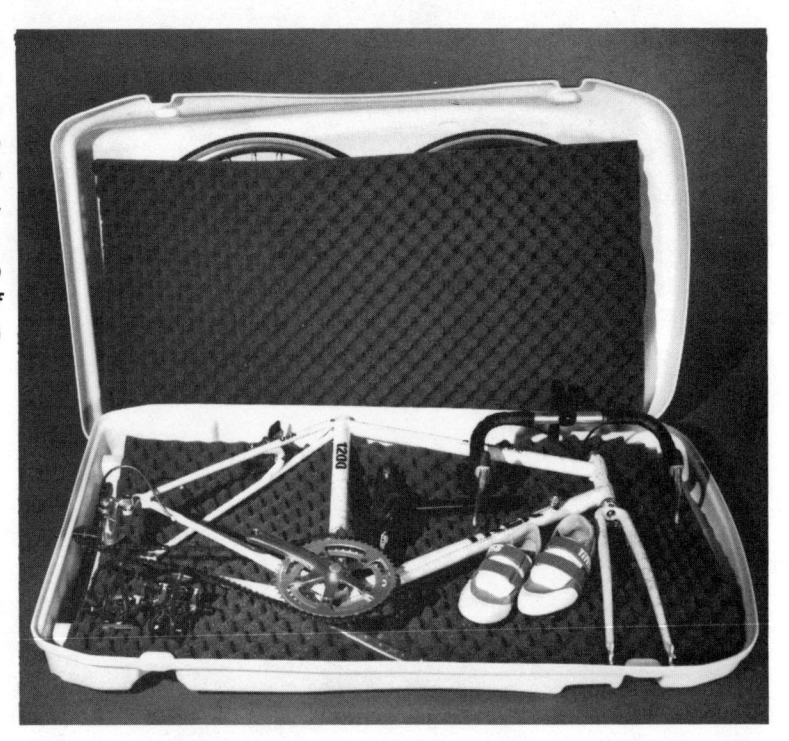

The box features a combination clamp, lock, and hinge, and can be opened from either side or the top can be removed completely. The interior features a high density foam to protect the bike. I think the GTI Box is probably the safest way to transport your bike. One feature I really like is the built-in wheels and handle, which make the box easy to roll so you don't have to carry it. Cost is in the $400 range.

Obviously, you may not always need as much protection as the GTI Box provides. There is a seemingly endless variety of racks to choose from.

Roof racks come in a few variations. The Graber Continental Upright Rack, for example, allows you to put the bike in the rack without removing the front wheel. Other roof racks involve removing the front wheel and clamping the fork into the rack. It is possible to transport quite a few bikes on the roof of your car with one of the racks that involves removing the front wheel. Roof racks cost between $150 and $500.

Rear racks clamp onto the back of a car and usually cost less than $100, although some of the rear racks that are capable of carrying two or three bikes may cost more.

If your car has an exterior spare tire attached to the tailgate, you may want to get a *spare tire bike rack*, which is a simple rack that slips over your car's spare tire. Cost is usually less than $60.

Front racks go on the front of your car and are also capable, depending on the model, of carrying two or three bikes. The one problem with front and rear racks is the bikes get a little beat up from road debris that gets kicked up from the highway. One solution is to buy a cover for any bikes that are exposed.

There are some *truck racks* made that allow you to carry bikes in the bed of your truck or inside a vehicle that has a fold-down rear seat and a tailgate. These racks involve removing the front wheel and then clamping the front fork into a quick release-type hub that is bolted either to the vehicle's floor or to a heavy board. If you own a large enough car to use this type of rack, you might want to give it serious consideration since the bikes are completely protected from outside debris (and theft).

Front car racks are capable of carrying two or three bikes.

These small under-the-seat pouches are ideal for keys, money, patch kits, and identification.

Whatever type of rack you get, make sure it is possible to lock the rack to the car ... and the bike to the rack. I know of one individual who went to great lengths to ensure his bike was locked to his car rack, but the rack wasn't locked to the car. You can guess what happened.

If you own a pickup truck, there are a few racks designed to clamp into your truck without any tools. These racks hold the bike upright and are usually relatively inexpensive, costing about $60.

If you are going to ship your bike somewhere and don't want to buy a case, take it to a bike shop to have it boxed. Or if you want to save money and do it yourself, here are some guidelines. Remove the front wheel and put a spare hub, or quick release mechanism with a piece of plastic, between the forks to keep them from becoming bent during transport.

Also remove the handlebars, seat and seatposts, and pedals. The key is to secure everything in the box so it doesn't move around during shipping. One common method is to tie the front wheel securely to the side of the frame.

Make sure to mark "This Side Up" on the box so that it doesn't get shipped upside down. Naturally, it's important to have your name, address, and phone number clearly written on the outside of the box. Also, put your name, address, and phone number inside the box in case the package becomes damaged and the labels are rendered illegible. Write "FRAGILE" on all sides.

ACCESSORIES AND CUSTOM EQUIPMENT   55

A "kiddie" cart is an excellent way to bring children riding with you.

CHILDREN'S SEATS AND TRAILERS

If you would like to take your child cycling with you, but she is too young to pedal, you might want to purchase one of the add-on seats or trailers designed to tow children.

Personally, I don't like add-on seats that clamp directly to the bicycle. If you fall, your child is going to fall, too ... possibly hitting the pavement with serious consequences. It always amazes me to see people zooming down the bikepath, barely avoiding disaster, with a child strapped innocently above the rear wheel. Cost for a child seat of this nature is generally less than $200.

A much better solution (in my opinion) is to use a trailer that has a swivel on it to prevent it from tipping over should the bike pulling it fall. In other words, if you crash and fall over, the trailer will stay upright. There are a lot of different types of trailers available, with cost ranging from $140 to well over $300.

Some features to consider are: what types of harnesses are involved, does it have a canopy to provide shade, and can it be detached and used as a stroller once you arrive at your destination. Most bike shops carry a few different models to choose from.

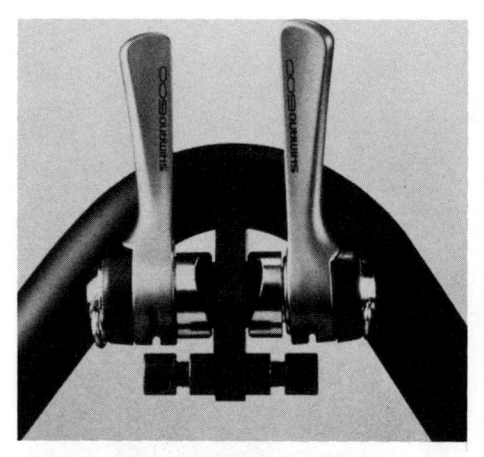

The AeroWave, made by Profile, is an excellent racing bar.

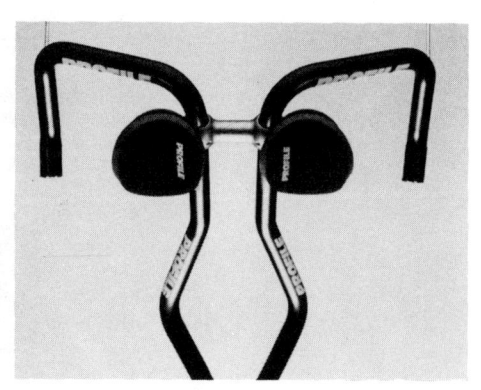

Placing the gear shift levers at the end of the aerobar is an ergonomic arrangement.

AEROBARS

Aerobars help you to obtain a more aerodynamic position on the bike and are ergonomically designed and comfortable to use. One common setup is to put the gear shift levers at the end of the aerobar so the rider doesn't have to shift his hand position to shift gears.

The AeroWave, made by Profile, is a good example and features positionable armrests, improved aerodynamics, and a lightweight design. It is also easy to install.

Quality aerobars, such as those made by Profile, are often a one-piece design and are made from heat-treated seamless aluminum. On the AeroWave bar, for example, the brackets are made from 6061-T6, which is an aircraft-quality aluminum.

For further information about Profile's excellent line of aerobars, contact:

Profile
6600 West Armitage Avenue
Chicago, IL 60635
(312) 237-5752

4
Safety

Cycling is a safe sport. Granted, if you spend a lot of time jumping your mountain bike or blasting down radical downhills, you may pick up a few bumps and scratches along the way. Even so, you will most likely ride home if you wear the necessary safety equipment.

If you plan to ride your bike on roads that are shared by automobiles, it is critical that you practice safe cycling. Something as simple as wearing a safety triangle (which can be bought for about $6) may make the difference between a motorist seeing you ... or rear-ending you.

HELMETS

This isn't an optional piece of equipment. Buy a helmet the day you buy your bike. This is a rule! *Always wear a helmet when you ride.* You may never fall off your bike—but if you do —wearing a helmet may save your life.

Mountain bikers are generally good about this and tend to always wear a helmet. It is road riding enthusiasts who are often caught without a helmet. This is ironic because one of the biggest risks to cyclists riding on the road is being hit by a car. If this happens, your body may have to absorb multiple blows. I know of one unfortunate cyclist who was hit by a car and thrown onto the car's windshield ... at which point the driver hit the brakes and slammed the cyclist off the car and onto the ground. The fact that this man was wearing a helmet saved his life.

You also need a helmet if you only ride on "car free" bikepaths. I think you are more likely to have a crash on a crowded bikepath than on the road. Where I live, crashes are all too common with inexperienced riders, high-speed road racers, and in-line skaters all sharing the same path along the beach.

The point is, *always wear a helmet*.

58 SPINNING: A GUIDE TO THE WORLD OF CYCLING

Always wear a helmet when cycling.

Riding without a helmet is dangerous. (Photo by Christine Lariviere.)

When you buy a helmet, make sure it is approved by either:

The Snell Memorial Foundation
P.O. Box 493
St. James, NY 11780
(516) 862-6440

or

American National Standards Institute
Safety and Health Department
1430 Broadway
New York, NY 10018
(212) 354-3300

The Snell Memorial Foundation is named after Pete Snell, a race car driver who was killed in a car crash in the 1950s while wearing a helmet that didn't provide adequate protection. The Snell Foundation now sets standards for helmets made for race car drivers, motorcyclists, and cyclists. Helmets that have been approved by Snell have a sticker with a serial number inside. The American National Standards Institute, known as ANSI, also sets standards for helmets. ANSI standards are not as hard to meet as Snell standards.

A quality cycling helmet will usually be approved by both organizations. Helmets made by Avenir, for example, state that they are Snell and ANSI approved on their box, making identification easy when shopping. Don't buy any helmet that isn't Snell and ANSI approved.

For information about Avenir helmets, write:

Avenir
4131 Via Pescador
Camarillo, CA 93012-9864

The three features to keep in mind when shopping for a helmet are:

Fit. Very important. If the helmet is uncomfortable to wear, you will probably start to "forget" to wear it. Make sure it feels comfortable when it's buckled up. Keep in mind that for the helmet to stay on your head during a crash, it has to be strapped on securely. Don't ride with the chinstrap loose and hanging an inch below your chin, or the helmet may get torn off your head on impact.

Ventilation. Bike helmets have holes in them to allow sweat and heat to escape. Avoid any helmet that doesn't feature some form of ventilation since it may be designed for another sport.

Weight. Cycling helmets are extremely lightweight. Avoid heavy helmets; they may be designed for another sport such as motorcycling.

Cycling helmets can cost anywhere between $20 and $100. Color often affects price. As long as the helmet is Snell and ANSI approved, it's safe.

EYEWEAR

It is very important to wear a pair of glasses when cycling. Small rocks, bugs, water, and other projectiles are commonly encountered at high speed. The first time one of these things bounces off your glasses with an audible "thud," you will appreciate the importance of the protection the glasses offer.

Oakley sunglasses are synonymous with cycling. They offer ultraviolet light protection, are plastic and won't shatter in a crash, and come in a bewildering variety of styles. Most of the lenses are interchangeable, and they even offer a clear lens for low light situations. Information about Oakley glasses can be obtained from:

Oakley
10 Holland
Irvine, CA 92718
(800) 733-6255

One of the things I like about Oakley glasses is the way they are designed to stay on your head without feeling like they're clamped on. Oakley glasses are very lightweight and comfortable.

Expect to pay between $40 and $150 for a pair of quality cycling glasses.

REFLECTIVE EQUIPMENT

There is a variety of equipment made to help motorists see you and your bike on the road. You should always ride with some type of reflective equipment—especially at night.

A *safety triangle* is a reflective triangle that hangs over your butt and is attached with a waist strap. It really makes a difference on the road. The large triangle helps you stand out to motorists while their car is still a few hundred feet away from you. However, it is not only for night use; a safety triangle

Wearing a safety triangle makes you more visible to motorists.

should be worn during the day, too, if you are riding in or around any type of traffic.

You can also buy *reflective tape* and put it on your clothing and equipment. The backs of your shoes are an ideal place for the tape because they are in motion and will catch a motorist's attention.

Your bike more than likely already has a few reflectors on it, usually above the wheels, on the wheels, and on the pedals. DON'T REMOVE YOUR BIKE'S REFLECTORS! If anything, consider adding more reflective equipment to yourself and your bike.

LIGHTS

If you are planning on riding at night, you should also put lights on your bike. Most bike shops carry a fairly wide selection to choose from, with prices ranging from $10 to over $200. You must have a headlight ... and I highly recommend you also get a taillight.

Keep in mind that lights should not be used in place of reflective equipment—they should be used in conjunction with it.

PROTECTIVE PADS AND CLOTHING

Knee pads, elbow pads, and gloves will definitely be appreciated if you come off your mountain bike. It depends a lot on how radically you ride. I don't jump my mountain bike much because I really dislike slamming into the ground. Since I tend to take it easy in the radical department, I don't wear protective pads. However, many of my friends love getting air, and they dress appropriately.

Gloves should not be considered optional. You can tear up the palms of your hands even on a slow fall from a stationary position. Don't ride without gloves.

REARVIEW MIRROR

You have a rearview mirror on your car; you should also have one on your bike. Being able to see what is coming up behind you is important. Granted, you can keep looking over your shoulder, but chances are, you won't do it as often as you will check a rearview mirror.

There are also times when it may be dangerous to look over your shoulder. For example, if a car unexpectedly pulls out of a driveway onto the road in front of you, the reaction time may not allow you the luxury of looking over your shoulder first. A rearview mirror could prevent you from swerving into another vehicle.

Some people can't look over their shoulder and ride in a straight line. The moment they look behind them, they begin to veer off course. The merits of a rearview mirror for these people are obvious.

Rearview mirrors are generally only used on road bikes or bikes that are used on the road. Off-road bikes don't sport rearview mirrors since you could become injured if you landed on a mirror during a fall.

HOW TO RIDE SAFELY

Riding safely really just involves common sense. Following are some of the concepts you should keep in mind.

Always Wear a Helmet

I know this is redundant, but the importance of it can't be overemphasized. If you crash, a helmet may make the difference between walking away or being carried away.

SAFETY **63**

Can you see the hole in the road in this picture? There is one about thirty feet ahead.

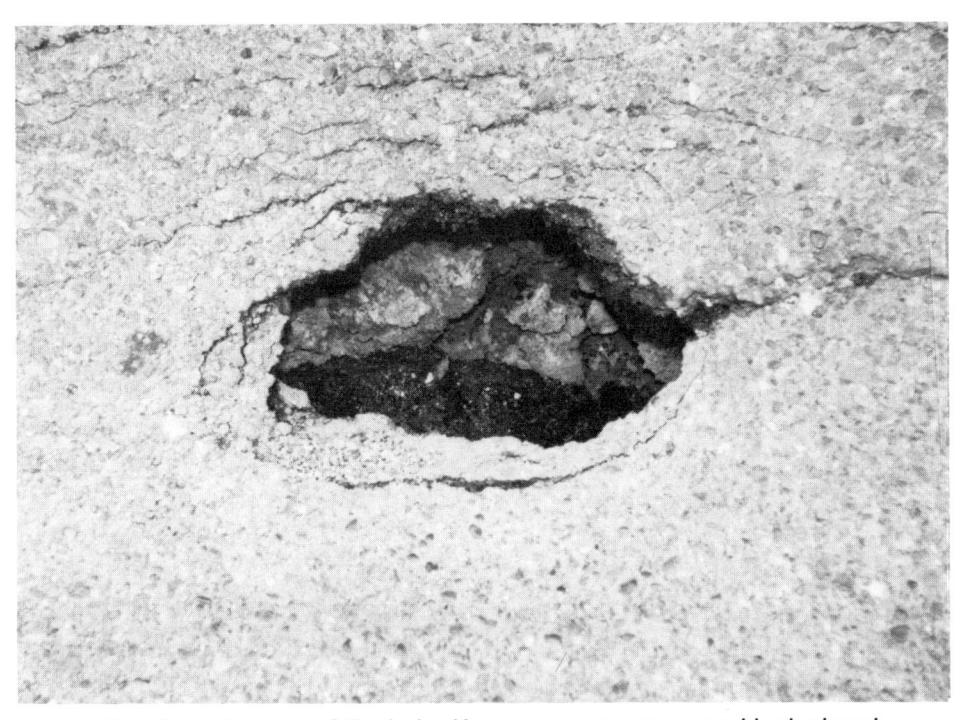

Here is a close-up of the hole. Keep your eyes open and look ahead when riding to avoid being surprised.

Always ride on the right side of the road and travel with the direction of traffic.

Always Wear Eye Protection

Protect your eyes from the sun's harmful ultraviolet rays and from foreign objects. As with a helmet, glasses should be considered part of your basic equipment.

Look Ahead

Don't just look for the obvious things, such as a moving car, but keep an eye out for other types of obstacles. For example, a dog that suddenly runs in front of your bike can lead to disaster if you hit it with your front wheel.

On the subject of front wheels, don't let anything jump, roll, or fly into your front wheel. I recently saw an unlucky cyclist go over his handlebars when a missed football pass slammed into his front wheel. (He wasn't hurt, but his bike was messed up a bit.)

Look ahead at all times and try to anticipate anything that might cause an accident. Keep a lookout for holes in the road, which may seem to appear magically in front of your bike. Creases in the road (such as where two slabs of cement meet) that run in the same direction you are traveling can be dangerous. The bike's front wheel can be pinched or "grabbed," throwing you off balance.

Loose gravel, dirt, and oil should also be looked for on the road since all can cause your bike to slip out from under you.

When in Doubt, Slow Down

If you see a situation developing, such as an in-line skater who is skating backwards and coming towards you, slow down.

If you are moving slowly, you are less likely to get hurt and you will have more time to react.

Incidentally, it's not uncommon to have to vocalize to get people's attention as you approach them. Keep in mind that your bike is a very quiet machine and people usually don't hear you coming. Be very careful when you are passing people on a bikepath or street, since they may not know you're there. If they "break left" as you pass left, it can be disastrous. To help avoid a collision, announce "on your left" as you approach to alert them to your presence.

Obey Traffic Laws

Behave on your bike as you would in a car. Use hand signals to indicate your turns and don't run red lights.

A sure way to anger a motorist is to hold up a "right turn only lane" by waiting for the light in the middle of the lane. If you are going straight, wait for the light along the side of the lane that continues straight.

Yield to Other Traffic

If you collide with a car, it won't matter who was right or wrong. Your body is going to be hurt more than the car. Don't assume a motorist will always acknowledge your right-of-way. If a car is making an obvious turn, let it go; it is possible the driver simply doesn't see you.

You should also yield to pedestrians. Remember, they may not see you coming. If you see someone about to step off a curb, try saying "hello" in a loud voice. If he doesn't seem to hear you, yield to him. Anytime a pedestrian isn't aware of you, yield. Keep in mind that you may also have to yield to pedestrians when you do have the right-of-way. Crashing into cars and people isn't fun. Fortunately, they are generally easy to avoid.

Ride Single File

Always ride single file on the road. You don't want to be "clipped" by a car as it passes you. Keep enough distance between bikes to allow plenty of reaction time should the person in front of you hit his brakes unexpectedly.

Hands on the Brakes

Anytime you are in a situation that might require sudden braking, keep your fingers on the brakes. For example, if you are weaving through pedestrians on a bikepath, be ready to brake. You might not have time to move your hands from the top of the handlebars to the brakes (not relevant on upright bars).

With upright handlebars, your hands are always in the right position to reach the brakes ... but you should still keep two fingers on your brakes if there is a possibility you might need to stop suddenly.

Don't Wear Headphones

This is actually illegal in some places. If you are listening to music with a set of portable headphones while you ride, you may not hear a car's horn or an emergency vehicle's siren. You don't want to collide with a fire truck because you didn't hear it coming.

Even if you only ride on "bikes only" paths, don't wear headphones. You won't be able to hear people coming up behind you.

Don't Ride Sick

Cycling is a physical activity. If you are not feeling well, don't ride. Something as simple as a cold can affect your reflexes, strength, and balance.

Riding a bike isn't only a matter of strength. It requires mental alertness, which can also be affected by illness.

Keep Your Bike Tuned

If your bike falls out of adjustment, get it fixed. Things such as rusted cables can lead to disaster if left untreated. Imagine having your brake cables snap while flying down a steep hill at thirty-five miles an hour! You most likely won't find the results fun.

Don't Ride Off-Road Alone

If you become injured while off-road riding, you may need assistance. A broken leg, for example, will make pedaling out under your own power impossible. Always ride with a friend.

Road riders are also safer with a companion, even though they are generally more likely to encounter assistance from other motorists, cyclists, and pedestrians. You are always safer riding with a friend.

Another reason to ride with a friend is to have assistance at hand if your bike breaks down. Most common problems can be fixed in the field, but what if something happens that renders your bike totally unrideable? A companion can go get help, spare parts, tools, or a car to transport you home.

5
Bike Handling Skills

This chapter isn't about how to ride a bike, it's about how to maximize your performance and efficiency on the bike. For example, what would you do if you were unexpectedly to encounter loose gravel during a high speed turn? Where you put your weight could make the difference between the bike holding the road or sliding out from under you. Acquiring a basic understanding of bike handling skills will give you the confidence to handle any situation you may encounter while riding. Knowing how to get the most performance out of your bike will increase your margin of safety.

OFF-ROAD RIDING SKILLS

Off-road riding generally requires a more specialized technique than road riding. Even so, much of the following off-road technique applies to all bicycles. In many cases, the technique is just more exaggerated when applied to off-road riding. Also, riding off-road is a great way to increase your road riding skills. All the sliding around in the dirt will improve your balance on the bike, which can really pay off on a slippery road down the line.

Descents

During downhill descents, get out of your saddle and move your weight back. Don't try to pedal unless you really need to. Stand on your pedals, keeping them horizontal so that your legs aren't uneven and you have a secure platform to stand on. The steeper the grade, the more you'll need to move your weight back.

If you are riding through a sharp turn, weight your outside pedal to avoid sliding out by pushing down as you lean the bike into the turn. Keep your body centered over the bike.

Practice your first high speed, off-road descents on easy terrain. (Photo by Christine Lariviere.)

Downhill Braking

Don't use your front brake by itself since it could send you over the handlebars. Apply the front brake simultaneously with the rear brake. Keep in mind that the front brake is what's going to slow you down the most since your momentum is forward. Don't slam on the brakes—apply them smoothly.

Don't ride the brakes. Holding the brakes during a descent is tiring since shock from the road gets transferred to your arms. Try to relax and let the bike "float" underneath you, using your arms and legs as shock absorbers.

When you need to use the brakes, don't brake hard or you will lock the wheels and start skidding. "Feather" the brakes to avoid becoming fatigued. Since you will be standing during most descents, it may help to move the brake levers into a more downward position to bring them more in line with your hands when you are in a standing position.

Don't try to descend anything that is beyond your skill level. As a novice, practice descending on hills that aren't too difficult or too steep, and give yourself time to develop your skills and confidence.

Picking a Line

It's important to *pick a line* and follow it. Plan well ahead and focus on where you want to go. Don't dwell on the ruts, rocks, and other obstacles. This is actually one of the keys to staying out of trouble. Plan well ahead and look for the clean line.

Don't get obsessed with an approaching trouble spot to the extent that you stop looking ahead. If you wait until the moment has arrived to plan your line around or over something, it's probably too late.

Using Speed

Bouncing, jumping, and ricocheting down a hill are easier than pedaling up, over, and around obstacles. Naturally, you shouldn't endanger yourself by trying something that is beyond your skill level, but keep in mind that it may be easier simply to go for it than to try to pick your way carefully down the hill.

Riding downhill slowly is often more fatiguing than going fast, since your arms are much more tense in a slow descent. Novices occasionally get in trouble when their arms become too tired to continue a slow descent, at which point they let go of the brakes and crash due to exhaustion. Spend some time riding down trails you are familiar with at higher speeds to increase your comfort level. However, try to avoid discovering something new (such as a large log) at a high speed in an unfamiliar area.

Dealing with Sudden Obstacles

It's likely that at some point during a rapid descent, you will suddenly spot a rock, branch, rut, or some other obstacle that could potentially throw you and your bike in an undesired direction. Dealing with these obstacles is relatively easy as long as you keep your cool and plan ahead. The trick is to lift your front wheel a moment before reaching the rut, rock, or fallen branch ... and then let your rear wheel bounce through, or over, whatever is blocking your way.

As you approach the obstruction, make sure your pedals are horizontal to provide a level base to stand on. Stand up and keep your knees comfortably bent, lean forward slightly, and prepare to throw your weight back to lift the bike's front wheel. Just before you hit the obstacle, throw your weight back and lift the bike's front wheel. The trick now is to maintain your balance as the bike's rear wheel bounces through, or over, whatever was in your way. Chances are you will catch some air.

Learning to jump and hop your bike takes lots of practice.

Landing can be done on both wheels or on the rear wheel. What you don't want to do is "endo" (land on the front wheel).

Front Wheel Lift

This is a useful skill that can be practiced anywhere. A wheel lift doesn't have to be a long distance wheelie; all you want to do is lift the bike's front wheel over an obstacle. There are two basic ways to lift the bike's front wheel off the ground. First, stand on the pedals, move your weight back, and simultaneously pull up on the handlebars to lift up the wheel. Second, use a hard pedal stroke in conjunction with pulling back on the handlebars.

In both cases, it may help to move your weight forward to "wind up" before throwing back your weight. Be prepared during your first attempts for the wheel to come too far up, tipping you off the back and onto the ground.

Your goal is to get the front wheel a few inches to one foot off the ground. Once you've developed a feel for it, find a *small* obstacle, such as a three- to six-inch log, and try to hop your front wheel over it. The goal is to keep the bike's wheel in the air as the rear wheel bounces over. Visualizing the maneuver in your mind as you are doing it may help. Don't think of it as simply pulling up the wheel, but as an arch that projects beyond the obstacle. Remember to keep your weight back through the landing.

This move has a lot of practical applications on the trail.

Learning to lift your rear wheel has a lot of uses in trail riding.

Letting your front wheel hit anything head-on may lead to an over-the-handlebars flight . . . which isn't fun. If you can at least get the bike's front wheel over an obstacle, the rear wheel will usually bounce over, provided you have enough momentum.

The Floating Turn

A floating turn involves turning the bike with the front wheel off the ground. It is an excellent way to make a turn in tight quarters. You can lift the wheel or bounce it off something to help get it in the air.

Find a mound of dirt or smooth rock to practice on. Hit the obstacle with enough momentum to help lift the bike's front wheel off the ground—be sure to keep your weight back. As soon as the wheel leaves the ground, lean the bike into the direction you want to turn and let the bike "fall" into the turn as you pedal.

Start by making small directional changes until you begin to get a feel for the maneuver. It's not necessary to lift the front wheel very high to make the turn.

You can make a floating turn by "bouncing" off almost anything. If there is not a "ramp" to help get the front wheel off the ground, execute a wheel lift as you approach the obstacle.

Rear Wheel Lift

To get your rear wheel off the ground, hit the front brakes as you shift your weight forward, and lift up with both feet.

The goal is to get the rear wheel a few inches to one foot off the ground. Practice at slow speeds, and be aware of the possibility of going over the handlebars. Grass makes a nice surface to practice on in case you fall.

Use a rear wheel lift to hop the back end of your bike around, a maneuver that is useful in trials competition. It's possible to make a stationary 180-degree direction change by alternately hopping the front and rear wheels around. Naturally, the goal is not to let your feet touch the ground. Learning how to lift the rear wheel also helps you develop a feel for what it is like to "unweight" the back of the bike. This becomes important when you want to learn to "hop" the entire bike into the air.

Weighting and Unweighting the Bike

If you ski, you are probably familiar with the concepts of weighting and unweighting your skis. The same concept applies to a bike you want to jump or hop.

To weight the bike, apply downward pressure by "jumping" down on the pedals. Keep the pedals level with each other to provide a stable platform.

Unweight the bike by suddenly standing up.

Jumping

The easiest way to learn to jump is to practice on a *small* mound or rise. The first few times, simply hit the rise with enough speed to get a feel for how the bike responds. Concentrate on keeping your weight back and the front wheel up—you don't want to land on your front wheel.

Once you have an idea of how much speed is needed to become airborne, try jumping upwards a little to unweight the bike as you lift the front wheel. Don't give an all-out effort, but proceed carefully. You don't want to launch yourself higher than you want to go.

Jumping can be a lot of fun, but it's also dangerous if you jump higher than your skill level can handle. Proceed slowly when learning, always wear a helmet, and make sure your bike is mechanically sound. (Imagine having your front wheel fall off in flight because you didn't check the quick release.)

Bunny Hop

A bunny hop involves getting both wheels off the ground without the aid of a jump or ramp. Basically, you do a front wheel lift and then immediately unweight and lift the rear wheel off the ground. The idea is to be able to clear an obstacle by

BIKE HANDLING SKILLS 73

Practice your first high speed, off-road descents on easy terrain. (Photo by Christine Lariviere.)

Don't jump or hop too high until you have a good feel for how to control the bike.

hopping over it without the bike's wheels touching it.

One of the keys to success here is to throw your weight forward after you lift the front wheel. This helps to unweight the rear wheel—remember to lift up with your feet as well. It's also important to stay in the air as the bike travels forward and over the obstacle.

Be sure you have enough forward momentum to clear the obstacle before you hit it; don't pedal during the maneuver. Practice hopping your bike without an obstacle before you attempt to clear something. Once you begin to get a feel for it, try clearing a *small* log.

It's possible to hop your bike several feet into the air from a stationary position. One of the most memorable cycling TV appearances was when trials champion Andy Grayson hopped his bike onto David Letterman's desk during an appearance on "Late Night with David Letterman."

Stationary Hops

Knowing how to hop your bike into a change of direction from a stationary position is extremely useful (and essential in some trials events). It's also a lot of fun and can be practiced anywhere.

The first skill you should practice and master is a *trackstand*, which is simply balancing the bike in a stationary position. You may want to keep your feet out of the toe clips in case you fall over during your first attempts.

Bring the bike to a standstill and lock the brakes. It may be helpful to turn the front wheel back and forth to aid in balance. If you are on a slope, make sure the front wheel is pointing downhill, which will make balancing easier.

You can practice balancing the bike off the trail as well. Stoplights are one opportunity, or just practice in your garage or a deserted parking lot.

Once you have mastered a trackstand, the next step is to learn to hop the front wheel. The move is basically the same as a wheel lift, but it requires more balance since you don't have any forward momentum. Forcefully push down on the handlebars to compress the front tire and immediately throw your weight back—pull back hard. Be aware of the possibility that the bike could tip over and dump you off the back.

Don't try to get the front wheel very high at first, but concentrate on landing and re-establishing your balance after the hop. Don't try any directional changes until you can consistently hop the front wheel and hold your position upon landing.

Once you can hop, land, and balance, try two hops or more in a row, rebounding on each jump to help you get higher the next time. Make directional changes by hopping the front end around on each jump. You will probably find it easier to alternate directions with each hop while you are learning. Try hopping back and forth.

It's also possible to change your direction from a stationary position by hopping the rear wheel around. Practice this maneuver on something soft, such as grass, since you'll have to be in the toe clips to lift the rear end of the bike and you might fall while learning.

Push your weight back and down to compress the rear tire. Instantly jump up and forward, lifting with your feet. Think of it as rotating the bike around the handlebars. Be extremely careful while learning this maneuver, because the possibility of being slammed forward onto your head does exist.

Practice a single hop followed by a trackstand. Once you have a feel for the maneuver, try doing a few consecutive hops and make directional changes as you go. The end goal is to make a complete 360-degree turn around the front wheel.

Once you are able to do front and rear wheel hops, try alternating them. It's possible to make a complete circle with the bike barely moving forwards or backwards. Trials competition often features 180-degree turns that can only be made by hopping the bike.

Spinning and Traction

Suddenly cranking down on your pedals when riding off-road can cause the rear wheel to break free of the dirt. The result is a tractionless spin that doesn't propel you anywhere. When you want to speed up, increase your cadence smoothly to avoid losing traction. Don't explode into a sprint in a sudden burst.

Zen Biking

If you stay rigid on the bike, every bump in the road will transmit shock to your body and you will tire quickly. Learn to let the bike "float" underneath you, using your arms and legs as shock absorbers. Visualize the bike as floating over the terrain and try to blend in with the bumps rather than letting them jar and knock you around. With a little practice, you'll become one with the bike ... and a lot more comfortable.

"Floating the bike" over rough terrain can also help cut down on the number of flats you get. If you are riding over a section of sharp rocks, for example, stay light on the pedals and unweight the bike as the tires pass over potential tire poppers.

You will also be able to react more quickly if you are in tune with the bike as opposed to being dead weight on the pedals. Try to "feel" what the bike is about to do the instant something begins to happen.

Stand Up

Sitting in the saddle over rough terrain can be a pain in the butt, not to mention the rest of your body, since every bump in the trail is transmitted through the bike to you. The solution is to stand up and use your arms and legs as shock absorbers.

A lot of off-road cyclists spend too much time sitting in the saddle when they should be standing. It's generally easier to balance the bike through difficult sections when you are in a standing position. You will also be able to sprint up small hills a lot easier in a standing position.

Why You Keep Your Bike in Good Condition

Don't ride your bike if something is wrong with it; your safety depends on your equipment. Nasty things can happen if a bike isn't looked over before a day's ride or after a fall. I once had my rear wheel fall off because the quick release had been knocked into the open position during a fall. Stupidly, I'd gotten back on the bike without looking it over first—a mile later, I was rear wheel-less.

The bike's chain is a potential trouble area for off-road riders. Always clean the bike's chain after a ride and keep it well lubricated. Carry a chain tool and a spare link with you ... these items might make the difference between riding and walking home.

On the subject of tool kits, always carry one off-road. A road rider may get away with a patch kit and pump if she is out for an afternoon ride; help is usually not far away. An off-road cyclist, however, must be self-sufficient. Going out without a basic tool kit can result in leaving your bike where it lies while you walk for help.

At the end of a day in the dirt, wash off your bike and then degrease and regrease the chain, derailleur, cogs, and chain rings. Check all cables and adjust them if necessary. Check that the wheels are true by spinning them and watching the distance between the rim and brake pads to see if there is a wobble. Check for loose spokes. Look over the bike for any signs of damage and tighten all nuts and bolts.

Tire pressure deserves special attention. Most off-road tires have a recommended off-road psi that is lower than the recommended paved surfaces psi. If the bike's tires are too full, they become mini-trampolines that bounce and jar you down the trail.

Make a point of keeping your tires at the low end of the recommended pressure for a more forgiving ride. A softer tire will also provide better tracking.

Stay Out of the Water

Stay out of water unless you plan to clean and lubricate your bike thoroughly as soon as you get home. I love riding through streams in Vermont ... and my bike has lots of rust to show for it. You will decrease the life of your bike if you allow water to get into its bearings. The easiest solution is to avoid getting soaked.

Mud is another culprit, although it's also a lot of fun to blast through mud. If you can, avoid riding in mud since your bike will pay a price. Once you get grit into the bike's bearings, you will have to live with that "grinding" sound until you dismantle and clean/overhaul them.

ROAD BIKE SKILLS

Sharp turns and steep hills merit some special consideration on a road bike.

Turns

Shallow turns at low speeds don't really require any special technique—you simply turn the bike. However, if you are traveling at high speed, and/or are making a sharp turn, you do need to apply some technique to succeed.

There are five things you should keep in mind:

Don't pedal. I've found that the best technique is to accelerate before the turn, and then coast through the turn. If you are riding fast, you may need to brake before the turn and then coast through it.

You shouldn't pedal during the turn for two reasons. First, your inside pedal may hit the ground as you lean the bike into the turn, and second, you should: *Apply downward pressure to the outside pedal.* Think of it as "pushing" the bike into the ground. Applying pressure in this manner can go a long way towards preventing the bike from skidding out from underneath you. Bikepaths and roads are often slippery. Water, sand, oil, dirt, and other hazards can cause a bike to slip out from under you. Applying constant downward pressure during the turns makes things much more stable.

Lean the bike into the turn. Leaning the bike to the *inside* of the turn works in conjunction with applying pressure to the *outside* pedal. Banking the bike should be done to make sharp turns. In fact, the only way you will be able to make fast, tight turns is to lean the bike over to steer.

Stay centered. Lean the bike *underneath* your body—don't lean with the bike. Stand up on the outside pedal and lean the bike to the inside. This is a much more stable way to turn since your weight is centered over the bike's tires. If you lean your body with the bike, the chances of the bike skidding out from under you are dangerously high.

Pick a line. It's important to look ahead before you turn and pick the line you will ride. Generally, the shortest and most stable line is to enter the outside of the turn, cut to the inside corner, and then exit to the outside again.

If you are riding through a series of tight turns and lose your line, don't try to "force" the bike back. Take a bit of time to slowly get back on your line as you glide through the next few turns. If you attempt to force the bike back in line, you may crash.

Riding Up Hills

Riding up a hill can be very tiring—especially if you do it without a bit of applied technique. In fact, many novice cyclists damage their knees through overextending themselves on steep inclines. To keep hills fun and to avoid hurting yourself, keep these tips in mind.

Use a lower gear than you think you need. One of the quickest ways to injure a knee that is new to cycling is to charge up hills in a high gear. Even if you feel strong, avoid the temptation. Use a low gear and save your knees. This is especially important if you are new to cycling. Also, by spinning in a low gear, you will save your strength for the rest of the hill.

Your uphill technique may change a little after a few months of riding. At this point, your legs and knees *may* have the strength to try shifting to a higher gear *after* starting up a hill in a low gear. Unfortunately, many cyclists do it backwards. They start in a high gear and "power" up the first part of the hill. As their strength dwindles, they shift to lower and lower gears, until they are exhausted and barely moving.

A much less stressful method is to start in a lower gear than you need, then shift to higher gears to pick up speed later in the climb. I've found this works really well because you don't tire out as fast and you stay stronger throughout the climb. Don't worry about the other cyclists who charge ahead of you in the early part of the climb. They'll almost certainly be running out of gas just as you start to accelerate.

Don't use the small gears on a hill if you are not physically ready. As a general rule of thumb, don't use any gear that you can't comfortably spin at 80 rpm or better. Certainly, don't use a gear that requires you to "muscle" up the hill.

Don't stand up on long hills. Pedaling out of the saddle requires more effort than pedaling in a sitting position. Your strength will last much longer on a long hill if you stay seated and try to relax.

Do stand up on short hills. Conversely, sprinting up short inclines is often easier if you stand up. The key word here is *short*. If the hill requires anything more than a short sprint, stay seated and shift to a low gear.

When you stand up on a short uphill sprint, *rock the bike* from side to side to help you generate rhythm and power as you pedal.

Sit upright. Most long hill climbs take place at fairly low speeds. Many cyclists find climbing easier if they hold the top of the handlebars. Since you are traveling at relatively slow speeds, a wind-resistant profile isn't really necessary. Sitting in an upright position allows you to breathe a little easier and helps you to stay more relaxed.

One way to judge how comfortable you are is to monitor how hard you are gripping the handlebars. A "vise-like" grip often indicates you are working too hard. Try to keep your arms relaxed. You don't want to use up oxygen keeping your upper body muscles tense. Save it for your legs!

Maintain a rhythm. This is important in all aspects of cycling. To help maintain a constant rhythm during a climb, it's important to *shift before the hill*. The idea is to maintain the same cadence on the hill as on the flats. The only way to make this happen (without blowing out your knees) is to shift in advance of reaching the incline so that you don't start pedaling slower as you start up the hill. If, when you start up the hill, you feel resistance that results in a slower cadence, either you timed it wrong or you are in too high a gear.

6
Training

Training isn't reserved for cyclists who are preparing for competitive events, tours, or organized recreational rides. All cyclists should use some kind of training program. At the very least, setting some long-range goals for yourself will help you to chart your progress. Also, a training program will keep your rides from becoming monotonous.

Training can take many forms and include a variety of routines. Long endurance rides, high speed intervals, recovery rides, pacelines, and cross-training with other sports are just some of the options available to recreational, serious amateur, and professional cyclists.

What follows are some general guidelines as to the types of training done by many cyclists. Keep in mind that there is an endless variety of training regimens being used by cyclists today. You may want to consult a coach who can design a program to meet your specific needs.

STARTING OUT: YOUR FIRST RIDES

If you are just starting out and haven't been riding at all, your first goal should be to work up to a ten-mile ride and repeat it three to five times per week. If you are overweight or haven't been exercising at all for a couple of years, consult a physician before beginning an exercise program.

Try to limit your first few weeks of riding to fairly flat terrain and don't use hard gears. It will take your body a few weeks to adjust to cycling, and you don't want to overdo it or injure yourself during this early stage.

Some people may find a ten-mile ride easy right off the bat. Only you can judge how many miles you can comfortably ride as a novice. Keep in mind that your goal is to repeat the regimen at least three times a week. It may be possible to ride thirty miles your first time on the bike, but then you may be too sore to ride again two days later.

Don't do anything that feels like it may be pulling muscles or straining your knees. It's better to take it easy in the beginning and slowly build your endurance and strength than to start pushing yourself hard before you are ready.

Once you have established a weekly mileage and routine, your next goal is to get your weekly mileage up to 100 miles. One hundred miles per week is a realistic distance for recreational cyclists who want to maintain fitness but have limited amounts of time.

THE IMPORTANCE OF WARMING UP

It is very important to give your body a chance to warm up before engaging in any strenuous exercise. Most cyclists take between six and ten miles at an easy pace to warm up. As a novice, ten miles may seem like a lot. In fact, your entire ride may only be ten miles long during your first few weeks of riding—although you will probably increase your mileage rapidly. Even if you are only riding ten miles at a time, take it slow and don't push yourself during your first few weeks of riding.

During the warm-up miles, try to maintain a consistent cadence in a gear that doesn't strain your legs or knees. Ideally, avoid a route with a lot of stops and starts. Bikepaths, for example, usually don't have nearly as many red lights and pedestrian crosswalks as street routes do.

Stretching prior to riding is an excellent idea. Start slowly and don't force anything. Gently stretch your muscles, holding the stretch rather than bouncing up and down. Stretching before riding can go a long way towards preventing pulled muscles.

INTENSITY

When limited time is a factor, some cyclists train with quality miles over quantity. For example, riding up a steady hill for twenty minutes at eighty percent of your maximum heart rate can be more beneficial than a slow, thirty-mile ride that barely raises your heart rate. Keep in mind that you must first spend a few weeks riding at an easy pace if you are a complete novice.

Occasionally, cyclists get into a routine of riding the same mileage every week at the same pace. Eventually, their level of fitness stabilizes and they no longer improve. If this happens to you, consider riding quality miles over quantity once in a while to put the sweat back into your workout.

I had this problem at one time while preparing for an endurance event. Each week was spent chasing mileage totals on relatively flat terrain. A few weeks into my program, I went for a ride with my hill-loving friend, Tom Maney, and was left hyperventilating in his wake after three miles of high-speed hill climbing. The lesson was obvious. Mileage isn't enough if you don't include some quality miles.

The Spin Coach, used by some cyclists seeking perfection of their spinning technique, is a stationary trainer that allows you to pedal with one foot. (Photo courtesy of Spin Coach.)

SPINNING

Riding a bike is easy, right? You simply pedal and go. Well, quite a few professional cyclists agree with that ... and quite a few don't. How a cyclist should correctly spin the pedals is a topic of serious debate for many coaches, competitors, and recreational cyclists.

One philosophy believes that proper spinning is only accomplished when one foot pulls up while the other pushes down. The concept is to eliminate the dead weight of the foot that is not involved in the down stroke.

On the other hand, many cyclists believe that this concept of pulling up with one foot is ridiculous. They cite the fact that the effort required to pedal with one foot tires out most people in under ten minutes.

Here is one analogy that seems to help many people who are trying to force their up stroke leg to do something constructive. Imagine that you are scraping mud off the bottom of your shoe when your foot reaches the downward end of its travel. The idea here is to create upward momentum. Perhaps the best thing that can be done is to "unweight" the leg that is along for the ride in order to eliminate drag. Basically, you will have to experiment to find what works best for you. Keep in mind that the up stroke "pull" is preached by some prominent racers.

CADENCE

Cadence refers to how fast you spin the pedals. One way to establish and keep track of your cycling rpm's is to buy a computer that has a cadence display.

What you want to do is learn to keep a constant cadence. One hundred rpm's is a good target for road riding; off-road riding often involves sudden changes in terrain, which can make constant spinning difficult.

Train yourself to spin easy gears fast and consistently. Condition yourself to spin at a consistent cadence, while making changes in speed with gear changes rather than with pedaling speed. Don't be lured, as many novices are, into pushing hard gears to increase speed. Concentrate on maintaining a consistent cadence.

A consistent cadence is also the best way to train your cardiovascular system because your heart rate will be sustained during the effort. Conversely, if you keep dropping the cadence, your heart rate will change accordingly and training won't be as effective.

Some riders seek to achieve a trance-like state to help them lock into a cadence. It helps to anticipate climbs so you can make the necessary gear changes in advance. What you want to avoid is having to slow down your cadence because you were late making the gear change before you hit the hill. It may help to get out of the saddle and sprint up small hills if you miss a gear change.

LACTIC ACID

Muscles use ATB (the body's power molecule) when working, which is provided from carbohydrates, oxygen, and fat stored in the body. Lactic acid is a by-product of working muscles. As lactic acid accumulates in a muscle, it interferes with the muscle's ability to draw energy. Fatigue and a "burning sensation" are the results of a high level of lactic acid in your muscles.

Avoiding the burning sensation associated with maximum effort is one way to keep your muscles below the lactic acid fatigue threshold. The best way to accomplish this is to ride just below the burn. Spinning easy gears at a high cadence instead of pushing hard gears slowly is an excellent way to forestall lactic acid buildup. This is another reason it is important to teach yourself to spin at high, consistent cadences.

Off-road riders may have a harder time preventing lactic acid buildup, since spinning at a consistent cadence is often difficult due to changing terrain and steep hills. High intensity interval training can help off-road riders by increasing their fitness level.

HEART RATE

Experts agree that the best way to increase aerobic fitness is to engage in exercise that raises your heartbeat to between sixty and eighty-five percent of your maximum heart rate. The basic theory is to exercise at least three times a week with the sessions lasting a minimum of twenty minutes.

What is your maximum heart rate? One of the most common methods of finding out your maximum heart rate is to subtract your age from 220. Keep in mind that this is a *general* figure; your maximum heart rate may be lower or higher. The best way to establish your heart rate is to have a doctor administer a stress test.

AEROBIC TRAINING

Aerobic conditioning is fairly easy to accomplish since the guidelines to training have been well defined for some time. Basically, you need to ride a minimum of three times a week for at least twenty minutes while keeping your heart rate at approximately eighty-five percent of your maximum heart rate.

Eventually, however, you will stabilize and need to increase the amount of time, effort, and/or frequency of your rides to improve. The important thing to remember is that you need to keep your heart rate up to benefit aerobically. A leisurely cruise along the beach may be fun, in addition to burning some calories ... but your cardiovascular system won't benefit much from the training.

INTERVALS AND SPRINTING

Interval training can be used to raise your anaerobic threshold (strength) and is an excellent way to develop explosive power in your legs. While aerobic training will strengthen your cardiovascular system, interval training will build power for sprinting. The concept behind interval training is to alternate riding at close to your maximum heart rate with recovery rides at roughly sixty percent of your maximum heart rate. Interval training can be divided up into long intervals and short intervals.

Short intervals could consist of a two-minute sprint followed by a five-minute recovery. A longer interval might consist of a five-minute sprint followed by a five-minute recovery.

Another way to train intervals is to cut down the length of the sprint and the recovery with each interval. For example, start with a three-minute sprint, followed by a three-minute recovery. Then do a two-and-one-half-minute sprint, followed by a two-and-one-half-minute recovery. Continue decreasing the time by thirty seconds with each interval until you get down to one minute. Then repeat the series five times. Keep in mind that these are general guidelines. Once you are familiar with the concept, you may want to design a program to meet your specific needs.

As with all training, use a heart monitor to ensure an accurate heart rate reading. It's important not to exceed your maximum heart rate during the intervals.

PACELINES

Pacelines are a fun way to train in a group and can be used to increase strength and sprinting power. They also give you the chance to ride much faster than if you were riding alone. A paceline involves riding in a line or group with riders trading the lead position every minute or so. The concept is for you to sprint to the front, where you must work harder in the lead position while your companions enjoy the advantage of being in the draft. Generally, the rider at the back of the pack sprints to the front and stays there for a predetermined amount of time ... at which point a new rider sprints up from the rear of the pack to take the lead.

Riding in pacelines is a good way to prepare for a race since you will learn the timing, effort, and strategies involved in taking the lead. If the group is riding fast, moving to the front can be very difficult. Conversely, if the pack slows down, take advantage of the lower speed and make your move.

REST

Some cyclists feel that it is beneficial to get off the bike for a week or two once or twice a year. I like to take a week off after a few months of intensive training to avoid burning out. After a week or so of not riding, it's very enjoyable to get back on the bike. Taking a break from your routine gives your body a chance to rest.

Some signs that you may be overtraining and need a break are insomnia, irritability, lack of focus, boredom, and constant soreness. Your resting heart rate is also a good barometer of your fitness level. For example, if your morning pulse rate suddenly becomes higher than usual, you may be overtraining.

RECOVERY RIDES

A recovery ride is used to let your body recover the day after a hard day of training. The idea is to go for a ride that is not too strenuous, and to ride at a pace that is comfortable. You want to give your muscles an opportunity to recover, but also keep them supple and loose. Many athletes ride longer distances than usual on their recovery rides, but at a non-strenuous and relaxed pace.

Training with a group of friends can keep your rides from becoming boring.

ENDURANCE

Endurance training is probably the easiest to accomplish—you simply increase the distance of your rides over time. Most cyclists have fairly good endurance after they have been riding for six months or so.

Keep a training log to help you keep track of each week's mileage. If you want to build up to a certain distance, increase your mileage by ten percent each week. The tricky part comes when you want to start increasing speed as well as distance. Interval training and other exercises can be included in your workout if you want to increase speed.

The hardest thing about endurance and distance training is finding time to complete your weekly rides. In a recent issue of *Bicycle Magazine*, Pete Penseyres, two-time winner of the Race Across America, recommends commuting to work each day on your bike to add miles. If you are training for an ultra-marathon type distance, using your bike for daily commuting will probably be essential to your training.

Another potential problem is boredom. If you are logging 200 or more miles a week, there will probably be times when you become bored and find it difficult to motivate yourself to ride. Some solutions are:

Ride with friends. Riding in a group can be social. Conversations can take your mind off the miles, and the distraction of fellow riders can go a long way towards eliminating boredom. Riding in a group also provides the opportunity for some friendly competition, which can help eat up the miles.

Pick a new path. Riding the same route day after day can get dull. Consider driving your bike to a new trailhead. Another possibility is to follow roads that you aren't familiar with. You may discover new sights that will occupy your attention. Another option is to ride at different times of the day to break up your routine.

Change your equipment. I've found that something as simple as a new pair of gloves can motivate me to ride. If you own both a road bike and a mountain bike, consider changing bikes for a while. You could even change to off-road trail riding for a week if you have been experiencing road burnout.

The twenty-four-day PAC Tour (for information about the 3,350 mile PAC Tour, refer to Chapter 10) obviously requires lots of preparation and endurance training. Tour organizer Lon Haldeman's training guidelines are provided below to give you an example of one possible endurance training program.

TRAINING **89**

Cycling should be fun. If you don't enjoy what you are doing, you probably won't stay with it.

A space shuttle bike.

Training Tips for the PAC Tour
General Goals for Overall Fitness

Within Three Months before the Tour:

1. Participate in six 100-mile or longer group events and be comfortable riding with others.

2. Ride 200 miles in less than fourteen hours with stops (a good gauge of PAC Tour fitness).

3. Be comfortable training 150-300 miles per week for ten weeks before the tour.

4. On two weekends, ride 100+ miles on Saturday and 100+ miles on Sunday.

5. Begin some of your training days at sunrise.

6. Ride in ninety-degree heat or higher as often as possible ... this is tough to do in April.

7. Ride the bike you will be using on the PAC Tour on your longer training rides. Get your shoes, cleats, arm supports, and saddle adjusted before the tour.

8. Be able to ride two miles in five minutes (twenty-four mph average), seven to ten times per week.

9. Veterans have found it is better to save up your limited training time and do two to three long rides per week (seventy-five to 100+ miles each) to get in your 200-300 miles per week instead of doing a casual twenty- to thirty-mile ride every day. When you do a shorter ride under thirty miles, try to maintain an eighteen to twenty mph pace. Most PAC Tour days are completed in ten hours, or at about fourteen mph with stops.

Three Months before the PAC Tour:

1. 150-200 miles per week.

2. One day per week over 100 miles.

3. One 150-mile, nonstop ride during the month.

4. Hang on the back of a fast group at twenty to twenty-five mph for thirty miles per week.

Two Months before the PAC Tour:

1. 200-250 miles per week.

2. Two days per week over 100 miles.

3. One 200-mile ride during the month.

4. Ride in the middle of a fast group for thirty miles per week.

One Month before the PAC Tour:

1. 250-300 miles per week.

2. Two days per week over 150 miles.

3. Ride a 200-mile event in under fourteen hours.

4. Ride in the front of a fast group for thirty miles per week.

One Week before the PAC Tour:

1. Ride enough to keep your legs fit, but stay rested and get plenty of sleep.

2. Overhaul and test ride your bicycle at least 100 miles.

3. Install a new narrow chain, a free wheel, and 700c x 25/28mm tires.

4. Pack your gear bag two days before you leave ... then take out half and leave it at home.

For more information about the PAC Tour, call or write:

PAC Tour
P.O. Box 73
Harvard, IL 60033
(815) 943-3171

DON'T BE REDUNDANT IN YOUR TRAINING

One sure way to get bored with your routine is to allow yourself to fall into a training rut. Don't always train the same way ... at the same speed ... for the same distance. You will benefit more, both physically and mentally, if you vary your training routine.

For example, if your goal is to ride 100 miles a week, vary the types of training you do each day. If Monday is an endurance ride of thirty miles over relatively flat terrain, consider doing some interval training over rolling terrain on Tuesday.

Wednesday could be used as a recovery day, when you go for a fifteen-mile ride at a leisurely pace. The point is, vary the intensity and types of training you do to keep interested and motivated.

TRAINING FOR THE PELOTON

Before you enter a race or a mass start event, it's a good idea to spend some time learning how to ride in a pack of cyclists. The only way to become accustomed to being surrounded by twenty or thirty other riders is to ride in a group and learn the skills required.

To begin developing the type of awareness needed when riding in a group, start off by riding with one other person. Spend time drafting behind him, keeping about six inches between your front wheel and his rear wheel. Remember to look in front of the other cyclist and be aware of the distance between your bikes. Take turns trading off the lead position with your training companion.

Next, practice riding side by side. This skill can take a little getting used to since most of us fear the other rider will swerve into us. Get used to being touched and bumped by a person riding next to you. Practice "bumping" under controlled conditions until you get used to it. It is actually possible to keep your balance and avoid crashing—even if you get hit hard.

Once you have spent some time training with just one other rider, start riding in a group of four or five people. Generally, roads shared by cars aren't a good choice, so look for large bikepaths or highways that have little to no traffic.

Pack riding often takes place at much higher speeds than cyclists obtain when riding alone. This means you must give yourself as much reaction time as possible in case something goes wrong. Don't dwell on the wheel in front of you, but look ahead and be prepared to take evasive action.

Practice catching the pack. Slow down and let the group gain a thirty-second lead, then sprint to catch them. This can be a type of interval training, resting in the draft of the pack once you catch them.

You might want to plan your group rides on days when you want to actively recover from a previous day's hard workout. As stated before, active recovery means taking it easy to let your muscles recover, while exercising. Riding in a pack can be fairly non-strenuous if you don't take the lead.

Incidentally, don't ever practice or try to develop strategies to block other riders. Sometimes you will hear competitors talking about cutting people off the road, or sandwiching them into the curb—all extremely dangerous and unethical. Don't buy into it! If someone is a better rider than you or has simply decided to attack when you haven't ... let her go. Don't ever block another competitor intentionally to make up for your lack of ability or speed.

SET GOALS

It helps to set both long-range and short-term training goals for yourself. Rather than aimlessly riding day to day—or even week to week—pick a long-range goal and then plan a training regimen to meet it.

Keep a training log and diary of your workouts. For example, let's say that you want to go on a week-long, 160-mile tour of the Canadian Rockies three months from now, but you are currently only riding forty miles a week. Plan a three-month program that ends with your riding 150 miles the week before the tour. Your program should include some interval training on hills to build strength and have a weekly mileage increase of about ten percent.

If you are getting ready for a specific race, outline a training program that will peak your performance the day (ideally) of the race. There are a lot of coaches who work with amateur athletes and can help you create a training program to achieve this.

Part of your training guidelines should be a list of the specific steps needed to achieve your goals. Distance alone isn't enough. Do you need to develop speed? Are you weak in the hills? Do you want to lose weight? Is your diet conducive to maximum performance? Are you getting enough rest?

Even if you are not preparing for a race or an upcoming tour, you should still set goals for yourself to chart your progress and help you stay motivated. Riding 100 miles a week over the same course at the same intensity will eventually get boring.

BREATHING

Breathe deeply and steadily when riding your bicycle. You want to avoid short shallow breaths, which can lead to dizziness. Lung capacity isn't really a consideration when cycling, since most people use only sixty to seventy percent of their total lung capacity. Even as you age, lung capacity isn't an inhibiting factor with cycling.

Don't worry about whether to breathe through your nose or your mouth, just do what feels natural. The most important thing is to stay relaxed and breathe rhythmically while you spin.

Keep in mind that when you are working hard, it's very important to breathe deeply to supply your body with the oxygen it needs to operate. Sometimes, a few deep breaths are all that is needed to generate a few critical powerful pedal strokes.

A group of professional racing cyclists at Springfield, Massachusetts, in 1886. (Courtesy of the Smithsonian Institution.)

Rudge racing Ordinary bicycle of about 1887, with its original owner, Godfrey A.S. Wieners. (Courtesy of the Smithsonian Institution.)

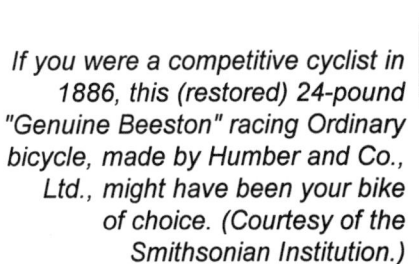

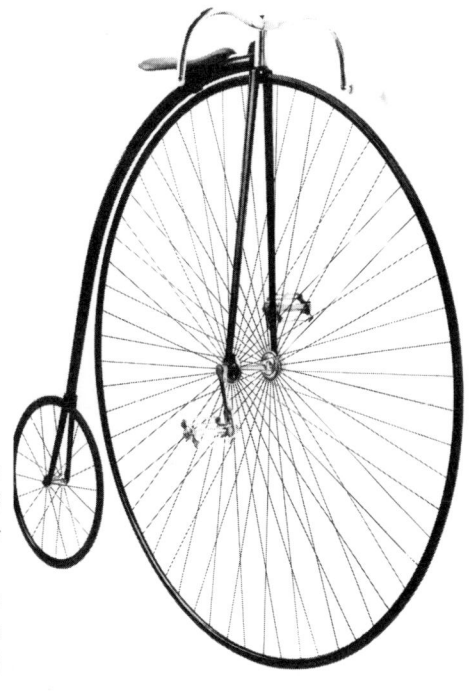

If you were a competitive cyclist in 1886, this (restored) 24-pound "Genuine Beeston" racing Ordinary bicycle, made by Humber and Co., Ltd., might have been your bike of choice. (Courtesy of the Smithsonian Institution.)

7
Racing

The design of the bicycle makes it ideal for racing since its propulsion relies solely on the strength of the rider. Being a mechanical device, there is lots of room for individual improvements in the bike's design and mechanics . . . and racing provides an ideal forum to test each new innovation. From the early hobby horse to today's state-of-the-art machines that can cost many thousands of dollars, bicycle racing has been a part of the sport from the very beginning.

Bicycle racing has been an Olympic sport since 1880, and it has evolved into many specialized disciplines. One appealing aspect of racing is that there is such a wide variety of events, almost anyone can find an enjoyable form of cycling competition. Don't think you would like competing against other people? Then the kilometer time trial, in which one rider rides on the track against the clock, may be just the thing for you. Endurance is something you might enjoy. Try competing in a 100-mile road race. High speed pursuits and strategies more to your liking? Then you will probably enjoy participating in a criterium.

WIND RESISTANCE/DRAFTING

Regardless of what type of racing you get into, one of the main things you will have to overcome is wind resistance. To overcome wind resistance, riders ride in the slipstream of the person in front of them. *Drafting* behind another rider is one of the basic strategies of bicycle riding. If someone is in front of you and going reasonably fast, he is blocking the wind for you. This is one of the most basic strategies in cycling—*it's easier to be behind someone than in front of him.* Deciding when to make your move to the front, and getting in the best position to make your move, is a big part of what racing is all about.

Racers Barczewski and Carney at the Lehigh County Velodrome in Emmaus, PA. (Photo courtesy of Lehigh County Velodrome.)

A competitor prepares to race the clock at the Encino Velodrome in southern California.

THE START OF A RACE

Getting a good start is important and may require some practice. I often practice starts during my training rides if I have to stop at a light and put a foot down.

If you are not being held, start with your strongest foot clipped in and slightly forward. If you start with the crank arm too high, there will be a slight delay when you start pedaling.

Clip your other foot in during its first down stroke. If you are using toe clip pedals and find that you are fumbling for a revolution to get your foot in, switch to clipless pedals. Fumbling with toe clips is a great way to lose time at the start of a race.

Think of the start as an explosion of power. Stand up in the saddle and stomp down on the pedals to blast off the line. You may find that your body suddenly goes way forward. Concentrate on not letting this happen and try to keep your butt over the bottom bracket. Also, don't rock the bike as you pump. Keep the bike upright and keep your butt over the center of the bike. It's also helpful not to look ahead but to focus on the road in front of your tire. Naturally, only do this for the first few strokes until you get up to speed. During a race—or anytime you ride—always look ahead. However, I find that looking down during those first few revolutions in a start helps me to focus. Visualize yourself as an explosion of power. The start is one time it may help to think in terms of "stomping" on the pedals for a few revolutions instead of spinning in a circular motion.

Keep your upper body still. This actually is a good idea most of the time you are riding. If you move your upper body around a lot, you're using up oxygen that should be going to the muscles in your legs.

Off-road strategies differ slightly from road and track techniques, and are discussed later in this chapter in the section on off-road racing.

PREVIEW THE COURSE

It's important in all races to preview the course. Off-road riders should actually try to ride the course before the race. Changes in terrain, obstacles, drop-offs, rollers, and other course particulars may require special bike handling skills. Practicing these maneuvers while you get to know the course is a lot easier if you are not also trying to nail down a winning time. Riding the course in advance will allow you to develop a realistic course strategy. There may be a section that you can't blast through without falling ... wouldn't you like to know about it in advance? Road racers should at least preview the course (often repeating a loop) by car to get a picture of the terrain. Taking a lap on the loop a few days before the race can give competitors a feel for how they should pace themselves during the race.

DEALING WITH FEAR

Fear can inhibit you during a race. Fear of conditions, fear of equipment failure, fear of limited skill, and fear of other competitors can all eat at a rider's confidence.

Fear can be healthy since it may prevent you from hurting yourself. However, if it's preventing you from performing to the best of your ability, you need to eliminate the problem. One of the best ways to do this is to increase your skill levels in the areas that are giving you difficulty. For example, if you are nervous riding in the center of a pack of forty riders, spend some time training in similar conditions that are slightly more controlled in order to build your skill and confidence.

Speed can also create fear. If careening down a hill at fifty miles an hour frightens you in a race, practice riding downhill during training rides at slower speeds. As your confidence and skill increase, pick up the pace.

Don't play a lot of "what if" games with yourself. Yes, it's possible to have your tire blow out at high speed, but worrying about it isn't going to help and it will probably affect your confidence and drive. If your concern about a possible event is so great that it's affecting your enjoyment of the moment and performance, perhaps you shouldn't be doing it.

VELODROME RACING

A velodrome is a racetrack for bicycles. Most tracks are three laps to a kilometer, although there are quite a few smaller four-lap tracks as well. The corners at each end of the track are banked to facilitate high-speed turns.

Riding in a velodrome is a wonderful pleasure. The banked turns are very natural since the bike stays perpendicular to the ground. One of the fears many people have about cycling is having the bike skid out from under them in a turn. Wet surfaces and roads with loose gravel on them can be particularly hazardous. In a velodrome, your bike is always perpendicular to the ground. It's a fun sensation.

There is a variety of races run at velodromes; some are

Olympic events. They are:

Individual Pursuit: Two riders begin at opposite sides of the track and pursue or chase each other. Winning is accomplished by either having the fastest time over the distance (usually between 2,000 and 4,000 meters) or catching the other competitor. The individual pursuit is an Olympic event.

Team Pursuit: A (generally) 4,000 meter race. Two teams start at opposite sides of the track and pursue each other. The team pursuit is an Olympic event.

Points Race: A pack of competitors rides around the track and sprints on designated laps (usually the fourth or fifth) to win points. The rider with the most points at the end of the race wins. The points race is an Olympic event.

Match Sprint: Usually a 1,000-meter race in which only the last lap is timed. The first part of the race is tactical, with riders jockeying for position before the final lap. The match sprint is an Olympic event.

Kilometer Time Trial: Riders race around the track individually against the clock. The rider who has the fastest time wins. The kilometer time trial is an Olympic event.

Keiren: A motorcycle or tandem bike paces riders around the track, increasing speed with each lap. Riders aren't allowed to pass the pace bike until it drops off before the final lap. The first part of the race is tactical, with riders jockeying for position before the final lap sprint.

Miss-N-Out: Also often written as Miss And Out. The last rider to cross the finish line on each lap must drop out. When only three competitors are left, they sprint for the finish.

Scratch Race: This is a simple race. The first rider to cross the finish line wins. Any distance can be designated.

Point a Lap: The winner of each lap wins a point. The rider with the most points at the end of the race wins.

Tempo Point Race: Same concept as a Point-a-Lap race, except that the first two riders to cross the finish line on each lap win two and one points respectively.

You may also encounter locally invented races or local variations on what is listed here.

Track Bikes

Track bikes, also called velodrome bikes, look like normal road bikes at first glance. A closer look, however, will reveal some startling differences.

Primarily, track bikes have a fixed gear—there is no gear shifting. You have one gear and that's it. This means you can't coast on these bikes. The pedals will always be moving if the rear wheel is moving. Additionally, there are no brakes on a track bike. Stopping is accomplished by circling the track until the bike loses its forward momentum and stops.

Once you get used to the techniques involved in riding a velodrome bike, you'll probably come to appreciate how simple and elegant they are.

Riding a velodrome bike on the road can be a great way to teach yourself to "spin" at a higher rpm. One racer summed it up well when he told a friend, "You can't make yourself do what these bikes will make you do."

The first time you ride one of these bikes downhill, you will understand why they can teach you to spin faster. In fact, you'll probably be spinning faster than you want to. When you ride a multi-speed bike, *you* decide how fast you want to spin the pedals. On a downhill run on a fixed gear bike, the *bike* decides how fast you will spin. (Naturally, it's very important you fit the bike with a set of brakes before riding it off the track.) Many cyclists find that this type of training teaches them that they can spin much faster than they had previously thought.

Training on a fixed gear bike is also great because most cyclists lack the discipline never to coast. A fixed gear bike will train you always to spin. You'll begin to forget about the concept of coasting and start spinning the pedals more consistently.

Velodrome Strategies

Velodrome racing can be extremely intense. During a road race, which may cover over 100 miles, cyclists benefit by riding with the pack and taking it easy in the early stages of the race. You often see road racers talking with each other or with their support personnel during the first part of a race. Conversely, in a points race, competitors are racing every few laps from the very start. There isn't any time to relax.

Many track racers feel that the sport is far more mental than physical. For example, strategies such as forcing a stronger rider to pass you on the outside during a turn, which results in him having to go a greater distance than you, can result in a slower rider winning a race over someone with stronger physical abilities. Many strategies are applied in the final moments of a sprint. It's not uncommon in velodrome racing to see a rider lead the pack for a series of laps, only to be suddenly overwhelmed by other competitors during the sprint laps. It's definitely a "thinking person's" sport.

One of the basic rules of riding in a velodrome is to *keep your eyes level with the horizon.* If you allow your head to bank in the turns with your body, you lose perspective on where up and down are, which can result in disorientation and a crash.

Another concept to keep in mind is to *always look ahead.* Don't focus on the rear wheel of the person in front of you. Remember, because you don't have any brakes, you need lots of reaction time. If you are focused only a foot or so in front of you, you'll probably overreact when you see something happen. It's just like driving a car—you want to take in the whole picture, not just the bumper in front of you. The way to avoid a crash is to see it well enough in advance to take evasive action.

Incidentally, many competitive cyclists feel that velodrome racing is the safest of all the competitive cycling disciplines. A road race may have downhill runs that involve speeds close to sixty miles an hour—a disastrous speed at which to crash. Also, you don't encounter unexpected obstacles on a track; you can see what is in front of you. A road racer has to deal with unexpected holes in the road, dogs, people—all of which may be encountered without warning.

For further information about velodrome racing, contact one of the following velodromes.

The Encino Velodrome
P.O. Box 16006
Encino, CA 91416
(818) 881-7441

Lehigh County Velodrome
217 Main
Emmaus, PA 18049
(215) 967-7587

Major Taylor Velodrome
3649 Cold Spring Road
Indianapolis, IN 46222
(317) 926-8350

National Sports Center Velodrome
1700 105th Avenue, NE
Blaine, MN 55449

7-Eleven Velodrome
1775 East Boulder
Colorado Springs, CO 80909
(719) 634-VELO

Alpenrose Velodrome
6149 SW Shattuck
Portland, OR 97221

Alkek Velodrome
18203 Groeschke
Houston, TX 77084
(713) 578-0858

ROAD RACING

Road racing is a psychological game of knowing when to attack and when to rest. For example, some competitors like to attack during the climbs, when a show of strength may be demoralizing to another competitor who is feeling fatigued. Another play is to stay on a rider's rear wheel as she increases the pace, letting her know you are unaffected by her show of speed by staying with her (seemingly) effortlessly.

If you are riding with people who are faster than you, try taking the lead during the climbs. Occasionally, other riders will accept the pace of the leader (as long as your speed is realistic) rather than pushing themselves to take the lead. If you let a stronger rider take the lead, he may increase the pace beyond your ability.

Conversely, staying behind a stronger rider without applying pressure can work to your advantage, too. He may accept your presence for the time being and consider you non-threatening—while you get the benefit of being in his draft.

There will be times when a show of strength works best. We all have days when we feel stronger than usual. If you feel strong, you may want to take the lead and force everyone to keep up with you. By pushing the other riders to catch you, you force them to think about what you're doing. It can be a psychological advantage since they will be aware that they are riding your race.

There may be opportunities to recover after attacks. Riding in the pack is one; another may be during the descents. For example, if you are tired after a long climb and there is a descent after the climb, try to sit in the saddle for a while. If you stand up during the descent, you'll be doing a form of isometric exercise by supporting your weight rather than sitting on your butt and letting your legs recover.

Drink lots of fluids during a race (and anytime you are riding). You may not feel like it, but you'll pay the price at the end of the race if you don't. The end of a race will be a 100-percent all-out sprint. You may be riding relatively easily in a pack for a large percentage of the race ... but the end will require everything you have.

If you don't drink throughout the ride, you will most definitely not be able to give a 100-percent effort at the end. More important, not taking fluids while you ride can result in serious health problems and even death.

It's important to pace yourself realistically, especially during a long race. If you are not in the kind of shape required to lead the field, don't do it. The important thing is to finish, and you don't want to run out of gas midway through the course because you started too fast.

There are a few different road racing events. They are:

Team Time Trial: Multiple teams (usually four riders to a team) ride against each other for the best time. A two-minute space is usually put between each time's start. The team time trial is an Olympic event.

Men's Road Race: A mass start event, often 124 miles over a repeating loop of ten miles (sometimes more or less). Road race distances vary depending on the type of event and the level of competitors for whom the event is designed. The road race is an Olympic event.

Women's Road Race: A fifty-mile race, usually also over a loop. An Olympic event.

Criterium: Criteriums, which are held in cities all over the country, are the most common form of road racing. The races are usually in the twenty-five- to sixty-mile range and consist of a repeating lap that is a mile or so in length.

Criteriums were created to simplify the amount of highway that has to be cordoned off for a bicycling race. Creating a fifty-mile course that doesn't repeat itself requires closing a lot of roads for the duration of the race. A criterium involves only one or two miles of road and doesn't inconvenience motorists so much.

"Crits" are usually fast-paced, spectator-oriented races. *Primes*, which are cash or merchandise prizes, are often rewarded for races within the race. For example, racers may compete on an individual lap, and spectators may also offer incentives to competitors in the form of cash prizes.

Stage Race: A stage race is held over a series of days. The Tour de France, for example, is a stage race that runs for several weeks. Riders compete to win each day's individual stage in addition to the overall race. It's possible for the overall winner never to win an individual stage. For example, winning one stage, but then finishing tenth on the rest of the days won't produce as good an overall score as finishing in second place in every stage.

Riding in the Peloton

Riding in a peloton (a pack of riders) is a thrill since you can obtain high speeds fairly easily—speeds that would require a lot more effort if you were riding solo. Being in a pack gives you the advantage of being in the draft of the riders in front. It's a lot easier to cruise at twenty-five miles an hour into a head wind if you are in a group than to go at it alone. Riding in the pack also gives you the opportunity to take a breather while you draft other riders.

However, there are some potential dangers when riding in a peloton—such as crashing and having twenty other riders pile up on top of you. To help avoid problems:

Grip the handlebars down so you can reach the brakes if necessary. You won't have time to switch hand positions if an emergency suddenly appears.

Stay near the front of the pack if you have the ability to get there. Generally, the better riders are at the front, which means it is less likely for an accident to occur there. If you get caught at the back of a bunch of novice riders, all crashing into each other, there's not much you can do.

Don't cross wheels. I made this mistake once while drafting someone. Suddenly he broke left, clipped my front wheel, and we both went down. Always leave a little distance between your front wheel and the rear wheel of the rider in front of you.

If someone bumps into you while you are riding, it doesn't mean you have to crash. If you do get accidentally "nudged" by someone—*don't panic*. Actually, it's surprising how many situations you can ride through simply by keeping your cool. If there is a need, get verbal and let the person know what's happening, keep your balance, and stay on the bike.

Competitors occasionally practice "bumping" while training. Getting used to the contact helps avoid crashes later.

The time may come when you decide to gently "bump" another rider who is crowding you. Don't do anything that might cause a crash, but a slight elbow nudge is often all that is needed to create a little breathing space between you and a pushy rider.

A motorcycle sets the pace at the Encino Velodrome during the keiren race.

Attacking and Breaking Away

Knowing when to break away from the pack is a skill that can only be developed through experience. Timing is everything. Break away too early, and you'll tire out and the pack will eventually reel you in and neutralize your effort. Conversely, wait until the end of the race, and there may not be enough distance or time left to gain a winning lead.

Many competitors make their moves during hill climbs when they sense other riders are tiring. For example, you and a small group may ride up a hill together ahead of the main pack. In addition, you might decide to break away from the lead group during the last moments of the climb. Confidence has a lot to do with it; you may feel stronger on some days than others.

People have individual strengths and weaknesses. While you may be strong on the hills, another competitor might be fearless and fast during the descents. After a while, you will probably become aware of other competitors' strengths and weaknesses. In addition to helping you decide when to attack, you may also want to "nurse" another rider's weakness so she will do the same for you. For example, if you are strong on the hills and are riding with someone who isn't, consider easing up slightly. When you reach the downhill, she may return the favor.

Most road races aren't won or lost during the first half of the race. Groups of competitors will often work together for the benefit of the group, saving the breakaways for the last half and the end of the race. Sprinting off for a strong lead at the beginning of a 100-mile race will often lead to defeat since you will probably tire out.

Be aware of what's happening with the wind in relation to the course. There is no point in making a breakaway into a strong head wind if the course turns downwind or cross wind a few miles later. Patience is often the key to making a successful breakaway. Let road conditions, race conditions, weather conditions, and other cyclists' attacks take their toll. Some competitors may not follow your breakaway if you make it during the second half of the race because they are already mentally defeated by the day's conditions.

The United States Cycling Federation is the governing body for road and track racing. Membership and additional information can be obtained by contacting:

The United States Cycling Federation
1750 East Boulder Street
Colorado Springs, CO 80909
(719) 578-4581

OFF-ROAD RACING

Off-road racing is an extremely physical sport. A cross-country mountain bike race is much more tiring than a road race over the same distance because *there is no rest* in the mountain bike event. Why? You can't draft behind another rider during an off-road course due to the conditions.

During a road race, the advantages of drafting are tremendous, especially if you are riding in a large pack of riders, since it allows you some rest during the race without sacrificing speed. In an off-road event, drafting is impossible for many reasons. For example, there are sections of the course where only one bike will be able to go through at a time. Also, mountain bike courses are rough—it's not possible to "sit" on another rider's rear wheel very efficiently. Another reason is that off-road racing involves a lot of jumps and obstacles. It's not at all uncommon to become airborne on downhill events, and falls are fairly common ... which can all be part of the fun if you are wearing the proper protective gear.

There are a lot of different types of off-road events. They are:

Downhill: A downhill run against the clock with a variety

of obstacles, usually about five minutes in length.

Dual Slalom: Two cyclists race head to head against each other through slalom gates over a downhill course (similar to skiing).

Uphill: The uphill event is usually the downhill course in reverse. There are both individual (the more common) and group start events.

Cross-Country: A cross-country course involves both uphills and downhills and a variety of obstacles and terrains. There are both individual and mass start events. The course distance is often in the forty-mile range, and it is usually a repeating loop.

Point to Point: A race from point "A" to point "B". This may be an individual or a group start event, and will usually feature a variety of terrains.

Trails: The point of a trails event is not to take your hands or feet off the bike's handlebars or pedals. Riders take turns riding over an obstacle course and are given a point (or points, depending on the fault) anytime their hands or feet leave the bike or they brush up against—or crash into—something. The rider with the fewest points wins.

Stage Race: A stage race is made up of a series of races. A three-day event, for example, might feature a cross-country race, a trials event, and a downhill on different days. Multiple event stage races require a lot of versatility.

Ultra-Endurance: To be classified as an ultra-endurance race, the course must be at least seventy-five miles long.

Off-Road Starts

Off-road races often start at high speed with riders sprinting full out. There are a couple of reasons for this. If the conditions are dusty, you want to get clear of the pack or you may end up riding in a dust cloud.

Another reason to get out in front early is if the trail narrows early on. The idea is to get ahead of the other riders before reaching the single track so that you can be in a lead position. Some competitors will sprint to the single track to obtain a leading position, and then slow down and rest since the people behind them can't pass. Above all, you don't want to get stuck in a traffic jam where a trail bottlenecks.

To make a fast break at the start, it's important to learn what gear works best for you. You don't want to start in a gear that will take a few pedal strokes to get going, nor do you want to be in too high a gear since that will mean you have to make a few shifts before you can get up to speed. Spend some time experimenting to discover what works best for you.

NORBA

The National Off-Road Bicycle Association, more commonly known as NORBA, is the governing body for off-road bicycle racing. NORBA is a nonprofit organization that sanctions off-road events worldwide. NORBA also supplies and trains race officials, helps clubs host events, sponsors clinics, is involved with securing public land access for off-road riders, and promotes responsible off-road riding habits.

Becoming a member of NORBA has many advantages, especially if you want to get into off-road racing. As a member, you will receive a NORBA license, accident insurance at their events, a twelve-issue subscription to *NORBA News*, an off-road competition guide, the opportunity to attend clinics, and a decal, and you'll be eligible to qualify for the National and World Championships ... all for about $25 a year. Even if you don't race off-road, you should become a NORBA member to support the work they do in obtaining trails and land for off-road cyclists. For information about becoming a NORBA member, contact:

> The National Off-Road Bicycle Association
> 1750 East Boulder Street
> Colorado Springs, CO 80909
> (719) 578-4626
> FAX: (719) 578-4628

To help make off-road racing enjoyable and fair, NORBA has a classification system that groups together riders of roughly the same age and ability. Your classification is stated on your license. The classes are as follows:

> Junior—12-18 years old
> Senior—19-34 years old
> Veteran—35-44 years old
> Master—45 and up
> Beginner—First Time or Casual Competitor
> Sport—Intermediate Competitor
> Expert—Very Advanced Competitor
> Pro/Elite—Top Level Competitor

THE RACE ACROSS AMERICA

The Race Across America, commonly referred to as RAAM, is one of the ultimate endurance events in the world. How long do you think a 2,909-mile race that starts in Irvine, California, and ends on the other side of the United States in Savannah, Georgia, would take?

Well, Bob Kish's winning time in 1992 was 8 days, 3 hours, and 11 minutes. Think about that for a few minutes ... and then if you would like to get more information about RAAM, call (714) 651-9913.

8
Cycling Health & Diet

How you treat your body and what you put into your body will directly affect how well it performs when cycling. While much of the general population abuses themselves with bad food and lifestyle habits, cyclists are generally well educated about what's good for them. Actually, manipulating your diet to maximize your performance is a big part of cycling at all levels. Even if all you do is go for a recreational ride a couple of times a week, eating correctly before, during, and after your ride will increase both your performance and your enjoyment.

Injuries are relatively uncommon in cycling. Except for crashing, which hopefully can be avoided (and the risk minimized with the proper safety equipment), there are very few ways to hurt yourself on a bike. Overall, bike riding is very safe.

Remember always to wear safety equipment such as a helmet and glasses; if you are off-road riding, also wear knee pads and any other safety equipment that may be necessary for your intended activity. The greatest risk of injury you will ever face on a bike is crashing into or colliding with something or someone.

THE IMPORTANCE OF WATER

Dehydration is one of the biggest potential problems faced by cyclists every time they go for a ride. Most athletes are aware that it is important to drink water when exercising. Surprisingly, however, many cyclists don't consume enough liquids while riding, which is dangerous because dehydration can lead to serious health problems, and can dramatically affect your performance. Consider the fact that you lose over a quart of water through sweat during an hour of moderate to heavy cycling. A recent study showed that this water loss cuts an athlete's endurance by twenty percent, and endurance and performance continue to decrease as your body becomes further dehydrated.

If you feel like resting during a ride ... do. It's important to listen to what your body tells you.

One of the reasons it is easy not to drink enough is that you don't necessarily feel thirsty when you need to drink. A good rule of thumb is to drink at least one bottle of water (a quart or more) for every hour of riding. Don't try to down the bottle all at once, but drink a little at least every fifteen minutes.

A headache is one symptom that you are not drinking enough while riding. Dehydration can also lead to heat stroke, which can result in death. Most professionally run events, such as triathlons and ultra-marathon cycling events, don't allow competitors to lose more than three percent of their body weight while racing. If you do lose more than three percent during a ride, you are definitely letting yourself dehydrate.

One important consideration is not to drink liquids that are too high in carbohydrates. Your body recognizes the high concentration of carbohydrates and processes the liquid as food, which slows down its absorption into your system. A solution is to water down any drinks that are exceptionally sweet.

Juice is good to drink during longer rides since it contains energy-creating carbohydrates. Water it down by at least *fifty percent* to ensure that the fluid is absorbed by your body at an acceptable rate. Avoid juices that can contain a lot of solids, such as orange juice, because it will take your body longer to deal with the solids. My personal favorite is Snapple™ pineapple juice because it is high in carbohydrates, tastes good watered down, is low in calories, and contains lots of vitamins.

LOSING WEIGHT

Cycling off the pounds is both easy and fun. Most people find that dieting alone is a difficult way to lose weight. If you combine diet with exercise, you'll find losing weight much easier. In fact, many people are amazed to find that they lose weight effortlessly once they start bike riding a few times a week.

Cycling has been proven to be so effective as a weight loss program that most gyms incorporate stationary trainers into their weight loss exercise programs.

How many calories does cycling burn? Well, factors such as speed, difficulty of terrain, and body weight all play a part in determining this. To give you a general idea, a 130-pound person riding fifteen miles an hour burns approximately 450 calories an hour. A 200-pound individual riding fifteen miles per hour burns approximately 675 calories an hour. Calorie consumption varies dramatically with body weight.

When you first begin to ride at regular intervals, your appetite will probably increase for a while. Don't worry about it — your appetite will decrease after a few weeks when your body has become adjusted to the increased activity. Actually, many cyclists have to force themselves to eat after riding to avoid weight loss and to replenish glycogen supplies.

Losing weight is simple. One pound of fat equals slightly less than 4,000 calories. To lose a pound of fat, you have to burn off almost 4,000 calories. For example, if the 200-pound person described above were to ride five and one-half hours (averaging fifteen miles per hour) per week, he would easily lose one pound a week.

Actually, most cyclists burn more calories and lose weight faster than what charts and graphs show. For example, riding fifteen miles an hour into a ten-mile-an-hour head wind will burn a lot more calories than riding without a head wind.

Keep in mind that as you lose weight, you also burn less calories per hour. You'll need to increase either your speed or your distance to continue to lose weight at the same rate. The good news is that your speed and distance will increase naturally as your fitness level rises.

My recommendation is that you don't worry about calories

at all. Simply start riding at regular intervals and plan a training program that increases your weekly mileage every few weeks. If you can get up to 100 miles a week, you will easily lose weight. Keep in mind that this program assumes you are not currently gaining weight.

If you are gaining weight, a cycling program will stop your weight gain, but may not result in weight loss initially. The good news here is that your appetite will decrease after a few weeks of cycling. It's a vicious, healthy circle that you will learn to love. The more you ride, the less you eat (after the initial adjustment period), the better you feel, and you begin to lose weight. I know this sounds simple, but I promise you it works! Just start bike riding and you will be amazed at how quickly your body will react to the exercise.

Cycling brings results fast in the areas of weight loss and toning. After as little as a week of cycling, you will see and feel results. Weight loss combined with body toning will result in you looking and feeling better in a relatively short period of time. So what are you waiting for? Start riding!

BACK PROBLEMS

Some cyclists experience back pain after long rides, which is ironic because cycling is often prescribed as therapy for patients with back problems. Generally, the cause of back pain when cycling is a poorly fitted bike. If you are having back trouble, consult a doctor to find out what is wrong. Also, check your bike for the proper fit.

Aerobars, which hyperextend the rider over the handlebars, are sometimes the cause of back problems. If you plan on riding with aerobars, make the transition slowly and give your body time to adjust to them.

A poorly adjusted seat can also lead to back problems. A friend of mine recently eliminated all back pain by moving her saddle forward slightly. Consult with a sports medicine specialist who is familiar with cycling to find a solution to your problems.

Off-road riding, which often involves a lot of jarring and pounding, can also result in back problems. If you are riding off-road a lot and are experiencing difficulties with your back, try riding on pavement to give your back a rest from the jarring of off-road riding.

The distance between your seat and handlebars can also have an effect on your back. Having to reach too far or being

CYCLING HEALTH AND DIET 117

Drink plenty of water when exercising to avoid dehydration.

Don't strain muscles and knees on hills that are beyond your conditioning. Walk the bike—you'll save yourself a possible injury.

cramped up are both causes of back pain. A new stem may resolve the problem if a minor adjustment is all that is needed. However, nothing can correct a bike frame that is simply the wrong size.

It may be possible to eliminate certain back problems through therapeutic exercises. Consult a physical therapist, who can instruct you in exercises to strengthen your back. Don't experiment on your own, since some forms of exercise can actually hurt your back and complicate the problem. Sit-ups, for example, can be very damaging if done incorrectly.

Most important, don't ignore a back problem. Consult a physician at the first sign of trouble.

NUMB HANDS

Some cyclists experience mild to extreme numbness in one or both hands during extended rides. Known as carpal tunnel syndrome (CTS), symptoms include pins and needles, weakness, pain, and most commonly numbness in the hand and wrist.

It's not uncommon for only one hand to experience numbness. For example, my left hand often goes slightly numb during extended time on the handlebar downs, while my right hand has never been affected. My solution is simply to return to an upright position and flex my left hand for a few moments. The movement involved in reaching for my water bottle and getting a drink is usually enough to restore feeling.

Causes of CTS include:

Squeezing too hard. The cause of carpal tunnel syndrome is usually pressure on the median nerve. Too much pressure on the hand and wrist, which may be caused by the bike's top tube being too long, can bring on CTS. The obvious solution is to make sure your bike is sized correctly. Seat position can also affect how much of your weight "falls forward."

CTS can also be brought on by squeezing the handlebars too tightly. Monitor your grip to see if this is the case.

The dominant hand is often the one that is affected, since cyclists usually don't remove it from the handlebars while they drink or make gear shifts. For example, I am lefthanded and my left hand is the one that is sometimes affected. Combat this problem by using your other hand to drink and make gear shifts. Obviously, don't do anything you lack the coordination for—you don't want to crash.

Wrist angle. Bending the wrists into an unnatural position may cause numbness. For example, turning your fingers to the side while resting your weight on your palms creates a severe bend in the wrist (and also limits your control of the bike). Riding the brake hoods can also result in weird wrist angles. Basically, if your hands are going numb, try a different hand position.

Moving your hands to a new position on the handlebars is often all that is needed to prevent problems. Road bikes offer more hand positions than upright handlebars. Experiment and see what works best for you.

Aerobars usually eliminate CTS because they align your arms, wrists, and hands, although they also limit your steering control.

Trail shock. Off-road riding, which usually involves a lot of bouncing and pounding, can result in CTS because riders often hang onto the bars with a death grip. Novice riders may find their hands tiring during descents because they are squeezing the handlebars too tightly.

The solution is to try to relax your grip in order to let the blood flow and to release pressure on the median nerve.

If the discomfort continues, consult a physician.

NUMB FEET

Numb feet and/or toes can result from a variety of things. Tight shoes, thin soles, and tight toe straps can all be causes.

If the toe straps on your toe clips are too tight, they can cut off the circulation in your feet, which will result in numbness. For example, some riders tighten their toe straps before a hill climb, and then forget to relieve the pressure later in the ride. If you are experiencing numbness, check your toe straps.

A too thin sole on your cycling shoes can result in the bottom of your foot, or your entire foot, becoming numb. The solution is to wear thicker socks or two pairs of socks, or to buy shoes with better padding.

Racing shoes often have thin soles since they are made to be as light as possible. Don't wear racing shoes during your training rides.

The cleat on clipless pedals may be felt through a thinly soled shoe. The cleat can often be moved slightly forward or backward, which may resolve the problem—as will a thicker soled shoe. Keep these potential problems in mind when shopping for clipless pedals and shoes.

As with any medical problem, consult a doctor if symptoms continue.

KNEE PAIN

Cycling is much less stressful on your joints than many other forms of exercise, but knee pain can become a problem if certain cautions aren't exercised. Don't ignore pain that doesn't go away ... consult a physician.

As with runners, cyclists whose feet turn in or out while pedaling can have knee problems. One solution is to get a pair of biopedals made to compensate for your specific condition. Biopedals can also compensate if your foot tilts to one side or the other. For further information about biopedals, contact:

Bio Sports
P.O. Box 111, 220 Redwood Highway
Mill Valley, CA 94941
(415) 388-2081

Biopedals can be set loosely so that they will automatically adjust to your specific needs ... at which point you can tighten them to hold the position. Another option is to have a local doctor "prescribe" the angle you need and send it to Bio Sports to be made. Or you can go to Bio Sports and be fitted in person. Dr. Halbac, who invented the biopedal at Bio Sports, explains that it is easy for individuals to adjust the pedals by themselves. Cost is $170.

Improper bike fit can also result in knee problems. The most common problem is having the bike seat too high or too low. Overextending the knee almost always results in problems. Seat position, frame size, stem length, and riding position can all affect a rider's knees. Make sure your bike fits you correctly.

Don't push hard gears, especially when going up hills or into strong head winds. Remember, it's better to spin easy gears fast than to spin hard gears slowly, which uses strength versus aerobic fitness. Straining the knees by pedaling too difficult a gear is probably the most common cause of knee problems.

Cross-training to strengthen your leg muscles can go a long way towards preventing problems. Weight training is particularly helpful since cycling tends to build up the quadriceps muscles, while ignoring the hamstring. Consult a trainer and tell him about your problem so that he can design a program specifically for you.

HYGIENE

It is important to get out of your cycling shorts as soon as practical after a ride. Avoid sitting around in sweaty bike clothes since this may result in skin rashes. If you are riding a lot, this is especially important because a nasty rash can keep you out of the saddle for a week or more. Skin rashes can also develop into saddle sores if left unattended. Consult a dermatologist if needed.

SADDLE SORES

A poorly fitted bike, an incorrect saddle position, lack of padding, and riding farther than you are conditioned for can all lead to saddle sores. Saddle sores generally come in two varieties. The first, and often most common, is a red rash that is sensitive to pressure. The second type is a little more serious and develops as a blister or open sore, and can be very painful.

One solution is to apply petroleum jelly to any trouble areas at the first sign of sensitivity. Many riders avoid saddle sores with petroleum jelly—called "greasing the baby."

Another solution is to increase the amount of padding between your butt and the bike's seat. Some cyclists wear two pairs of padded underwear as a solution. Keep in mind that you should still correct whatever it is that's creating the problem. Something as simple as changing the angle of your seat may be all that is needed to alleviate the problem of saddle sores.

NATURE'S HAZARDS

Any activity that takes place away from civilization has certain risks. Fortunately, very few of these are encountered by off-road riders. Unless you practice bunny hopping your bike on top of a rattlesnake, you will probably never get bitten, be stung, or encounter anything poisonous. However, just to be safe, you should become familiar with what to do if you encounter something hazardous.

Stings from bees are probably the biggest risk to cyclists, since we occasionally slam into them at high speed. Aggravate a wasp by hitting him with your face at twenty miles an hour ... and you might get stung. The only consideration with bees is that you remove the portion of the stinger that may be left in your skin. Be sure not to squeeze the sack of poison that may be present.

If you get bitten or stung by something you can't identify that causes pain or discomfort—or creates a strange-looking rash, lump, lesion, or any other type of sore—consult a doctor immediately. It's possible you may have been bitten without knowing it. Some spider bites, for example, take a few days before they become painful.

If a snake bites you, the good news is that you will definitely be aware of it. Should you be unfortunate enough to be bitten by a poisonous species, seek medical help immediately. It's important to stay calm and to keep your heart rate as low as possible. You don't want to help the venom pump through your body.

Many experts feel that snake bite kits shouldn't be used. The concern is that some people do more damage to themselves with the scalpel these kits are supplied with than the venom does. You can have a friend attempt to suck the venom from the wound (but not if the friend has any open wounds in his mouth, and he must spit the venom out), but don't hack at yourself with a scalpel. Get medical attention immediately.

Incidentally, if possible, kill the snake and bring it with you so that medical personnel can identity the species to aid in selecting a suitable antivenin. Don't endanger yourself or a companion trying to kill the snake, but if it's possible, bring the snake in for identification.

Some off-road riding areas have poisonous plants. Learn to identify poison oak, poison ivy, and anything else you shouldn't touch. Some people are much more allergic to these plants than others. Keep in mind that scratching an area that has been infected will spread the rash. There are some nonprescription drugs to treat these types of rashes, but you may need to see a doctor if you are highly susceptible.

Don't eat anything on the trail that you aren't 150 percent sure is safe to consume. Just because it looks like a berry doesn't mean it is edible. I have a friend who insists I sample the various leaves, berries, and other so-called edible trail snacks when we ride together. I always decline because I once witnessed him vomit one of his trail snacks.

If you suspect you've eaten something poisonous, seek medical attention immediately. As with some types of bites, symptoms may not appear for a few hours.

DIET

Here lies the secret to successful cycling. More than anything else you do, what you eat can make or break your training, racing, and recreational riding. Fortunately, the dietary guidelines for cyclists are fairly well defined and easy to follow. The basics are a diet made up of seventy percent carbohydrates, fifteen percent protein, and fifteen percent fat. Bicyclists as a group tend to be far more educated than the general population in regards to knowing what is good for them and how to manipulate their diet to achieve peak performances.

Carbohydrates

Carbohydrates are a cyclist's best friend since they are a primary source of energy. "Carbo loading" the day before, or for a few days before, a race or big ride is beneficial because it loads your muscles with glycogen, which your muscles use for fuel. The result is that you have more strength and endurance and are able to perform more efficiently.

Eating foods high in carbohydrates after exercising is beneficial—in fact, essential—because carbohydrates replace the glycogen burned during exercise. After a two-hour ride, you have burned up most of the glycogen in your muscles; eating carbohydrates puts it back.

What you want is food that is rich with carbohydrates, but low in fat. Pasta is one of the best, making it an ideal food for cyclists. For example, three and one-fourth cups of pasta will supply you with 150 grams of carbohydrates, but only four grams of fat. You would have to consume twelve slices of whole wheat bread to get the same amount of carbohydrates available in the pasta.

The trick to not consuming a lot of fat is not to put a lot of heavy sauce on your pasta. Some sauces, such as the cream-filled alfredo and carbonara sauces, are so fat heavy that they outweigh the benefit of the pasta. Stick with plain sauce and toppings such as tomato or primavera.

Eat after You Ride

It is common knowledge that the body is able to replace glycogen most efficiently during the two hours after you finish exercising. Take advantage of this window by eating and drinking carbohydrates after you ride. Consider this: a study in the *Journal of Applied Physiology* showed that athletes who consumed carbohydrates immediately after exercising replaced glycogen three times faster than athletes who waited more than two hours to eat or drink.

Eating after you ride isn't as important if you are not planning to ride again for a couple of days. However, if you are planning to ride the following day, your performance will be directly affected by the amount of glycogen your muscles have been able to replace.

124 SPINNING: A GUIDE TO THE WORLD OF CYCLING

Cyclists can burn up a lot of calories, so it's important to eat the right types of food after a ride. This isn't one of them.

Cycling is excellent for overall conditioning.

How many carbohydrates should you consume? Most nutritionists recommend consuming half a gram of carbohydrates for every pound of body weight after a hard ride. The common practice is to consume half this amount directly after riding ... and then eat again about an hour later.

Discovering how many grams of carbohydrates a food contains can be difficult unless you take the time to read labels and have a nutritional guide. Another option is to count calories, although this method isn't as accurate. As a guideline, remember that one gram of carbohydrate equals about four calories.

Eat on the Bike

After about two hours of effort on the bike, your body's glycogen supply has been depleted. Consuming carbohydrates at this point generates energy by providing glycogen to power muscles. A variety of sport drinks supply carbohydrates in addition to vitamins and minerals. These drinks are good choices for on-the-road beverages.

For extended efforts, bring along some snacks to eat while riding. Energy bars are terrific since they contain carbohydrates but are low in fat. My favorites are Power Bars, which come in a variety of flavors.

Bonking is a term used to describe what happens when the body's glycogen stores have been depleted and carbohydrates haven't been consumed. Bonking can be dangerous because it often results in less oxygen going to the brain as muscles in the legs begin to struggle for energy. Symptoms are lightheadedness, fatigue, and lack of concentration. Most riders "bonk" if they don't consume carbohydrates during rides that exceed two hours.

Remember, anytime you feel your concentration drifting away, or you feel a little dizzy, you are probably beginning to bonk and should stop and rest in addition to drinking and eating something.

Protein

Protein is used to build body tissue and is an important part of your diet. Unfortunately, some cyclists become so engrossed in consuming carbohydrates that they forget about eating protein. The result is usually low energy and poor performance.

I occasionally like to eat a protein-rich breakfast before a long ride. Pancakes, which are high in carbohydrates and are one of the standard cycling breakfasts, sometimes leave me feeling empty early in a ride. I prefer a full breakfast of eggs, meat, toast, and pancakes. Some coaches and pro cyclists also believe in the protein-high breakfast before a big ride, although most nutritionists disagree and feel that carbohydrate-rich foods are the way to go.

Many nutritionists feel that cyclists don't consume enough protein, which is why they suddenly start feeling better when they consume a protein-rich meal. Keep in mind that the U.S. Recommended Daily Allowance for protein isn't enough if you are riding a few hundred miles a week. To calculate how much protein an active cyclist should consume, many nutritionists recommend multiplying your body weight by 0.54. However, eating too much protein can lead to health problems and should be avoided. Sound confusing? The best solution is to consult a nutritionist, who can create a diet to suit your specific needs.

Don't wear your helmet back like this. Make sure it fits snugly on your head and that the chin strap isn't loose. (Photo by Tom Maney.)

9
Maintenance and Repair

It is important to become familiar with some of the basics of bicycle repair because it's unsafe to ride a bike that is out of adjustment. Actually, there is no reason to ride a bike that is in need of repair or maintenance since it's easy to make most of the adjustments yourself.

The most common mechanical problems can usually be quickly remedied with a few simple tools. Why suffer the annoyance of a derailleur that keeps throwing the chain off your bike when you could eliminate the problem by turning a screw?

Most cyclists enjoy working on their bike. You don't necessarily need a workshop. My workshop, for example, is in the back of my truck.

Many repairs and adjustments, such as raising or lowering the handlebars, can be made in the field.

TOOLS

Before you can give your bike a tune-up, you will need to buy a few tools. Actually, most of the tools needed are fairly basic and you may already own some of them.

Chain Rivet Extractor

A *chain rivet extractor* (or "chain tool") is used when you want to add or delete a link in your chain or replace the chain. When you put a new chain on your bike, it's important to lay the old and new chains next to each other and count the links, since chains stretch with use. You want to have the same number of links in your new chain as in the old chain. Use the chain rivet extractor to add or remove links if necessary.

You may occasionally need to replace a broken link in your chain. To avoid breaking down on the road, carry an extra link and chain tool in your spare parts/tool kit. An inexpensive model will cost under $10, with deluxe models in the $90 range. Ease of operation is what you get in the upper price ranges.

Chain Whips

Chain whips are used to remove the free wheel and outer sprocket. One whip is used to hold the rest of the sprockets in place while you twist off the small cog and free wheel (depending on the model) with the second whip. This operation isn't something you would commonly do on the road (hopefully), so most cyclists don't buy chain whips. A chain whip will cost you between $10 and $20.

Spoke Wrench

A *spoke wrench* is used to remove or tighten the spokes on your bike. If you are planning on touring without any type of support, you should carry an extra spoke and a spoke wrench. A spoke wrench costs under $10.

Truing Stand

If you want to build a wheel, or realign and balance a wheel, you will need a *truing stand*. A truing stand is used to hold the wheel while you spin it to see which side of the rim is out of alignment. Cost is between $60 and $450—there's quite a range of models.

Y Wrench

Named after its shape, a *Y wrench* is a useful tool for dealing

MAINTENANCE AND REPAIR 129

A chain rivet extractor is used when you want to remove or replace a link in the bike's chain.

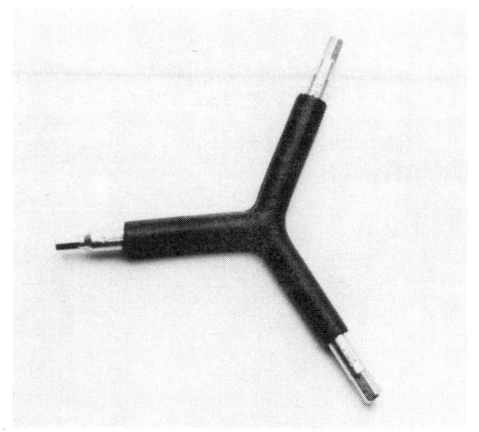

A Y Wrench is a useful tool to have on the road. (Photo courtesy of Derby Cycle Corporation.)

Cone wrenches are usually sold in a set of two. One wrench is used to stop the wheel's hub from turning while you adjust the opposite side with the second wrench. (Photo courtesy of Derby Cycle Corporation.)

This portable bike stand costs less than $15, gets the rear wheel off the ground, and is ideal for quick roadside repairs.

130 SPINNING: A GUIDE TO THE WORLD OF CYCLING

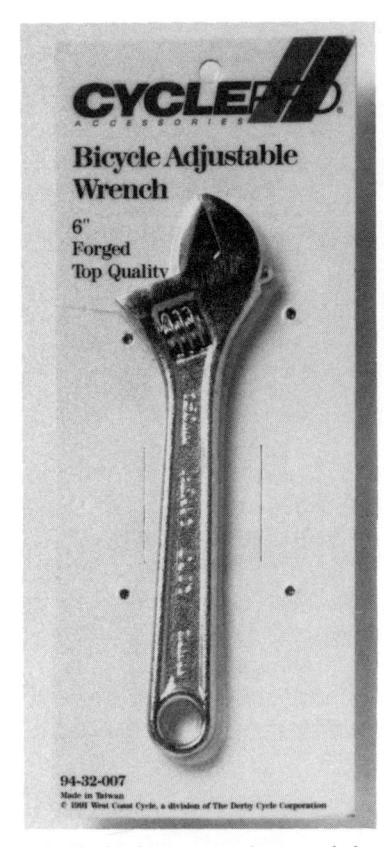

A six-inch crescent wrench is one of the basic tools of bicycle repair. (Photo courtesy of Derby Cycle Corporation.)

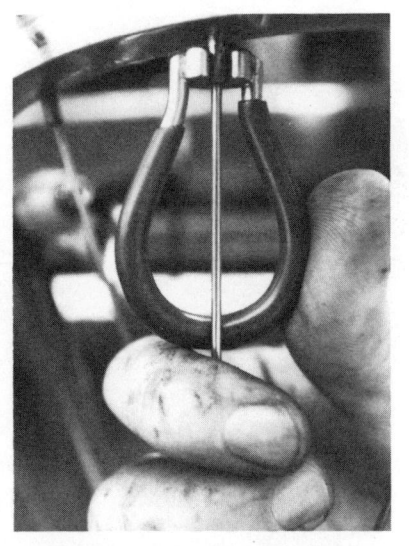

A spoke wrench is needed to adjust a bike's spokes.

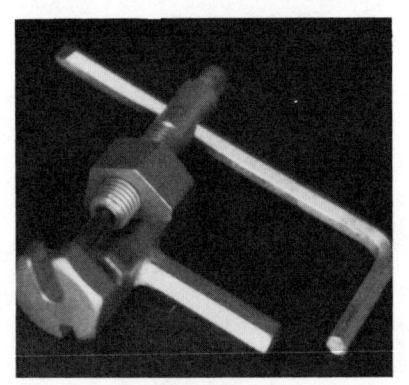

Multi-use tool has a chain rivet extractor, allen wrenches, a spoke wrench, and a screwdriver in one unit. (Photo by Trail Tracker.)

This basic tool kit includes (from top left) 8, 9, and 10mm Y wrenches (or whatever size your bike uses), allen wrenches, a spoke wrench, a chain rivet extractor, a six-inch crescent wrench, a cone wrench, tire irons, and needle nose pliers. The second set of allen wrenches is extra.

with the various nuts and bolts on your bike. Y wrenches come in different sizes and types, so you should obviously get one that fits your bike's nuts and/or bolts. Price is under $10.

Allen Wrenches

Even if you are not planning to do any repairs or maintenance yourself, you will still need a set of *allen wrenches* for minor "comfort" adjustments—such as raising or lowering your seat, or adjusting the forward angle of your seat.

Get one of the combination tools that have all the sizes you will need in one unit. These tools often have screwdrivers built into them, which is useful. Cost is usually under $10.

Crescent and Open-Ended Wrenches

A six-inch *crescent wrench* is useful since most bikes use a variety of different size nuts and bolts. You'll also need a big wrench to fit the lock nut on your bike's headset. Wrenches can cost anywhere from $5 to $40, depending on size and quality.

An alternative to crescent wrenches is to buy a few *open-ended wrenches* in the various sizes needed to work on your bike. This is only practical for a home-based workshop.

Cone Wrenches

Cone wrenches are thin wrenches used to adjust the cones in the hubs (center of the wheel) and pedals of your bike. You will need two cone wrenches to make adjustments. Cost is generally under $10, although it's possible to pay over $20 for a "deluxe" wrench.

Tire Irons

Tire irons are a must. Even if you don't buy any other tools, buy a tire iron and patch kit (or spare inner tube) and carry these items with you when you ride.

Lightweight plastic tire irons can be bought in "3 packs" for under $10. The reason three are needed is that you may need to pry the tire out of the rim with one or two irons while you run the other iron around the rim to unseat the rest of the tire.

Needle Nose Pliers

A pair of *needle nose pliers* comes in handy whenever you are dealing with cables. Both the brakes and derailleurs are controlled with cables that occasionally need adjusting. Needle nose pliers are also useful when you have to hold a small nut or bolt in place. Cost is in the $10 range.

Screwdrivers

You will need both *slot* and *Phillips head screwdrivers*. Take a look at the size and type of screws on your bike to determine exactly what size you should buy.

Small screwdrivers are useful things to have on the road in case you need to adjust something. Limit screws, for example, which adjust the derailleurs, require small screwdrivers. Many of the combination allen wrench tools also include small slot and Phillips head screwdrivers. Expect to pay between $5 and $20.

Bike Stand

Some type of *bike stand* will be necessary since you will need to get the rear wheel off the ground and pedal the bike with your hands while you make certain adjustments. You'll also find removing tires and other jobs a lot easier to perform with the bike in a stand.

Some portable stands cost less than $15. These types of stands hook onto the bottom of the bike and lift the rear wheel off the ground. They are ideal for quick, in-the-field repairs, or for "removable" workshops if you have limited space at home. A large stand can't be conveniently tucked away in a small apartment.

Larger stands can easily cost over $100. They offer the convenience of getting the entire bike off the ground and are usually equipped with tool trays and other features. The larger stands also free you from bending over to work on your bike since they hold the bike at about waist level (height is adjustable on many models).

Third Hand

A *third hand* is basically a clamp that is primarily used to hold the two sides of a brake together while you adjust the cable. A third hand also comes in handy during other jobs — whenever you need a "third hand."

Lock Ring Spanner

"Spanner" is just another word for wrench, and the two words are often interchanged with each other. A *lock ring spanner* is used to remove or adjust the lock ring on the bike's bottom bracket. Make sure you get one that is the correct size for your bike. Cost ranges between $6 and $40.

Pin Wrench

A *pin wrench* is also used on the bottom bracket. Most adjustable cups require a pin wrench to remove or adjust them. As with all the tools you buy, be sure to get the right size for your bike. Cost is in the $15 range.

Some bottom brackets require special tools. For example, Sun Tour's sealed bottom bracket can only be adjusted with a tool designed specifically for the job. If you're unsure as to what your bike needs, tell the salesperson (or show him) what you own before buying specialty tools.

Fixed Cup Wrench

You will also need a *fixed cup wrench* for your bottom bracket ($15). Some manufacturers sell a set of "bottom bracket wrenches" consisting of a fixed cup wrench, a pin wrench, and a lock ring spanner. A set of wrenches may cost $60.

Crank Extractor

To remove the crank arms, you will need a *crank extractor*, which is a wrench used to reach the recessed bolt that holds the crank arms in place. Expect to spend between $10 and $20.

Cable Cutters

Cable cutters are needed for the brake and derailleur cables. Some tools are also designed to cut the plastic cable housing without pinching it at the ends. Price ranges from $20 to $60.

Free Wheel Remover

There are a lot of different size *free wheel remover* tools made to fit the various types of free wheels in use. Make sure you match the tool to your bike. Cost is usually in the $10 range.

FIXING A FLAT TIRE

Fixing a flat tire is easy ... and knowing how to change a flat can prevent a long (perhaps many miles) walk back to your car, house, or bike shop. Always carry tire irons and a patch kit (and/or spare tube) when you ride. These items are lightweight and small enough to fit in a pouch under the bicycle seat.

Although there is a variety of types of tires used on bicycles, *wired-on tires*, which consist of an outer tire and an inner tube, are the most common. For that reason, only directions for repairing wired-on tires are discussed.

To fix a flat:

134 *SPINNING: A GUIDE TO THE WORLD OF CYCLING*

It may be necessary to use one or more tire irons to hold the tire out of the rim. Use a third iron to free the rest of the tire.

Start on the opposite side of the valve and pull the inner tube out of the tire.

Remove the wheel from the bike. If you are dealing with the rear wheel, first shift the chain onto the smallest (outermost) cog before you remove the wheel.

Most modern bikes use *quick release levers* to attach and remove the wheels. However, some wheels on inexpensive models and most track bikes are attached with *axle nuts*, which require a wrench to remove.

Inspect the tire. Look over the tire to see if you can locate what caused the flat. If you find anything, remove it so that a new puncture isn't created after you repair the flat.

Unseat the tire. Use a tire iron to pry and unseat the tire from the rim. Start opposite the valve stem.

It may be necessary to attach one or two tire irons to a spoke to keep a section of the tire out of the rim while you use a second or third iron to unseat the rest of the tire. Some tires can be unseated with only a single iron or tire tool.

Only unseat one side of the tire; leave the other side tucked in the rim. It's not necessary to remove the tire from the rim to change the tube.

Remove the tube. Starting opposite the valve stem, pull the tube out of the tire. Remove the stem from the rim last.

Take note of the *rim strip* that runs around the inside of the rim. Its function is to protect the tube from the spokes.

A friend of mine, Justin, recently went touring through Holland. On the first day of the trip, he had five flat tires! The reason, he later discovered, was that the rim strip was too thin and didn't offer adequate protection. If you find you are getting an unusual number of flats, check the rim strip.

Occasionally, a spoke (especially if it's a replacement) may protrude into the tube. If you find this is the case, file it down.

Find the hole. Pump the tube up and listen for the leak. Although often not practical in the field, submerging the tube in water is an excellent way of locating leaks.

Patch the hole. Your patch kit should consist of glue, patches, and a piece of sandpaper. Lightly sand the area around the hole with the sandpaper, then apply some glue and let it dry until it's "tacky." Put the patch on and remove the plastic covering from the patch.

One option is to carry a spare tube (cost is usually less than $5) when you ride. This way you won't have to deal with patching the hole. Keep in mind, however, that you may get a second flat. Even if you have a spare tube, it's a good idea also to carry a patch kit "just in case" ... especially off-road.

After you have put a little air in the repaired (or new) inner tube, begin to put it back in the tire by first putting the valve stem through the hole in the rim and rim strip.

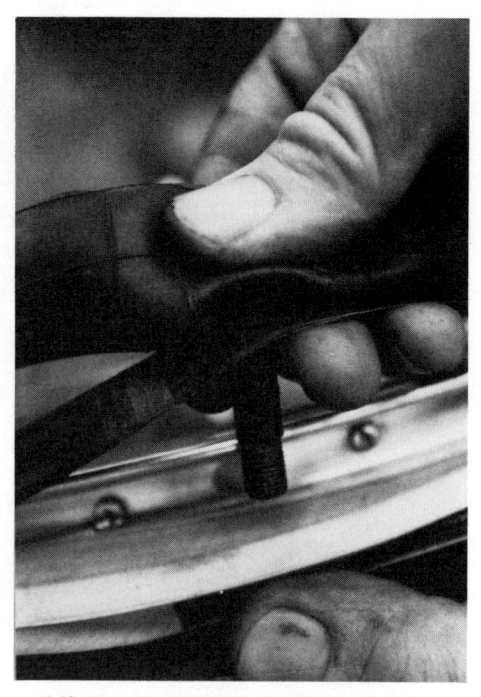

Lift the rim strip away from the rim when you put the stem valve through it.

Once you have put the inner tube back in the tire, start at the side opposite the valve stem and tuck the tire back into the rim.

Inspect the inside of the tire. This is an important step since whatever punctured your tube may still be in the tire. *Carefully* run your fingers around the inside of the tire, feeling for any type of foreign object. Remove anything you find.

Put the tube back in the tire. First put a little air in the tube. Start by putting the valve stem through the hole in the rim strip and rim. Lift the rim strip off the rim and put the valve stem through its hole first, then push the rest of the tube into the tire.

Reseat the tire. Starting opposite the valve stem, tuck the tire back into the rim. End with the area around the valve stem.

Fill the tire. Pump up the tire about halfway and check for "bubbles," or lumps, caused by the tube being pinched inside the tire. If you find a bubble, unseat the tire and straighten out the tube. If you don't find any bubbles, pump up the tire and reinstall it on the bike.

DERAILLEUR PROBLEMS

Your bike has two derailleurs that may occasionally need adjusting. The front derailleur moves the chain from one chain ring to the other chain ring; the rear derailleur moves the chain from sprocket to sprocket as you shift.

Derailleurs are adjusted with limit screws and barrel adjusters.

Limit screws are used to set the maximum throw of the derailleur. These two small screws are usually located next to each other, with one marked "L" (for low) and the other "H" (for high). Think of the "H" screw as also meaning "hard" to help you remember that it is used to adjust the small sprocket side of the derailleur's throw (as in hard to pedal).

Limit screws are used on both the front and the rear derailleurs. For example, if your chain comes off when you shift onto the big chain ring, the derailleur is probably moving the chain too far to the "outside." Use the "H" screw to set the derailleur's maximum throw until it is lined up exactly over the big chain ring. Conversely, if the chain were to keep coming off the smallest chain ring (towards the center of the bike), you would use the "L" screw to set the derailleur's maximum throw.

Adjust the limit screws one-half turn at a time. The idea is to line up the chain ring (or sprocket), chain, and cage of the derailleur in a straight line.

Barrel adjusters are used to adjust the cable tension of the derailleur. There may be as many as three barrel adjusters

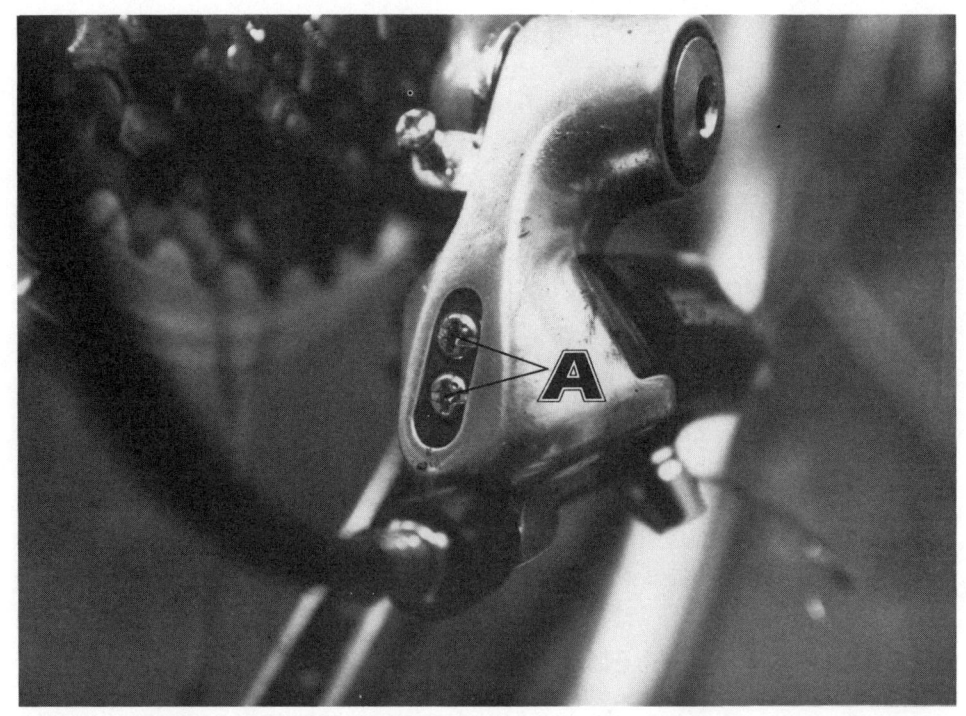

Limit screws (A) are used to adjust how far the derailleur can travel.

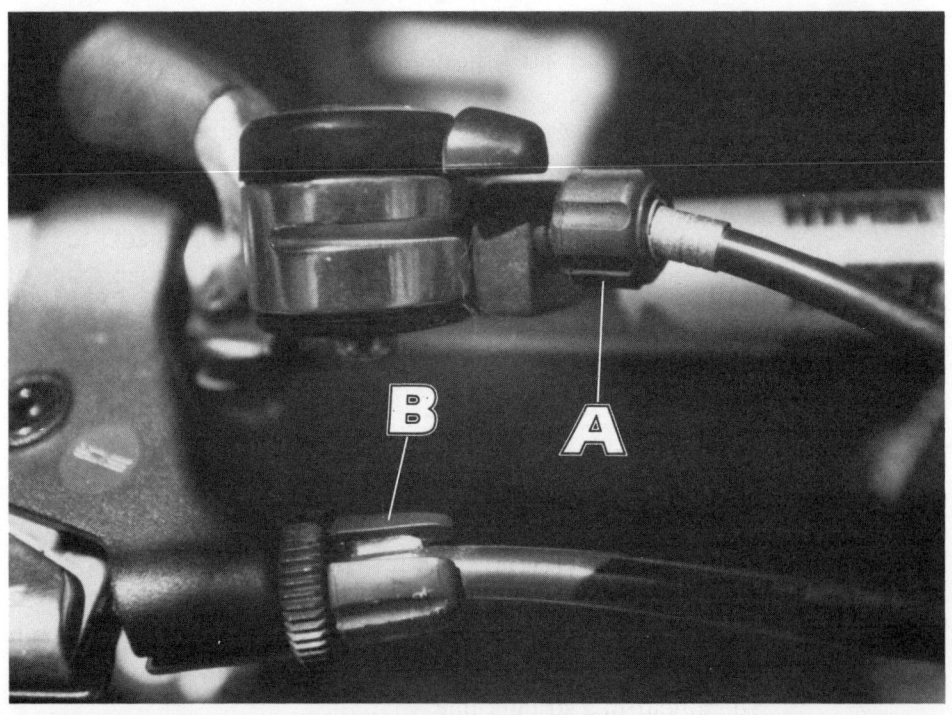

Barrel adjusters are used to adjust the brakes (B) and the derailleurs (A).

MAINTENANCE AND REPAIR 139

Adjusting the hubs on your bike involves first loosening the lock nut (A), and then adjusting the cone (C). A washer (B) will usually be found between them.

mounted at different locations along the cable. You tighten the cable by backing out the barrel adjuster. Loosen the cable by going the other way. In most cases, the cable will need to be tightened.

For example, if your chain is "jumping" back and forth between two sprockets or is making a grinding sound, tightening or loosening the cable by turning the barrel adjusters will usually solve the problem. You will need to have the bike in a stand that gets the rear wheel off the ground while you make the adjustments. Pedal the bike with your hands and play with the barrel adjuster until the problem is fixed.

If the barrel adjuster is all the way out and you need to tighten the cable farther, loosen the bolt that clamps the cable in place on the derailleur and pull it tight with a pair of needle nose pliers. Put the chain on the smallest sprocket and biggest chain ring before you do this.

Keeping your derailleurs and chain clean can go a long way towards keeping them trouble free. Use a degreaser to clean the chain, chain rings, derailleurs, and sprockets. Put a little degreaser on a rag and also clean the pulley wheels and cage of the rear derailleur.

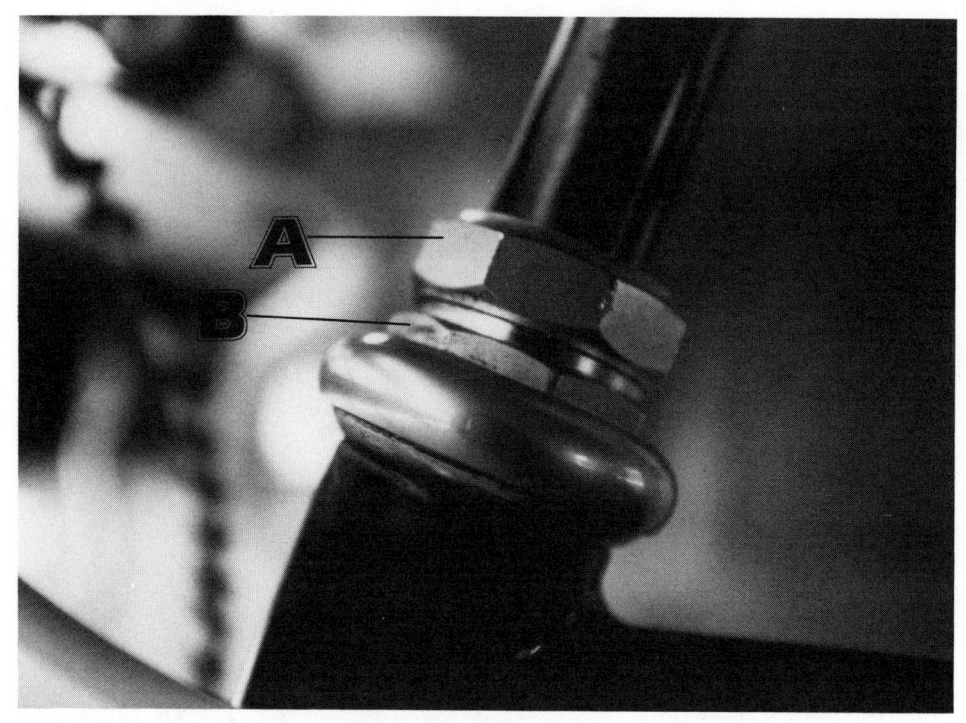

Adjusting the bike's headset involves first loosening the locknut (A) and then adjusting the adjustable cup (B) underneath.

STEERING PROBLEMS

The two adjustments you may need to make on the steering system are tightening the headset, and raising or lowering the handlebars. The steering system is made up of the front forks, the upper and lower headsets, the stem, and the handlebars.

Adjusting the Headset

If your bike develops a bit of "wobble" or play in the steering, you will need to tighten the upper headset. First loosen the locknut until the washer underneath it can be lifted a little. The idea is to gain access to the adjustable cup underneath the washer.

Once you have access to the adjustable cup, tighten it until the steering is no longer loose. Retighten the locknut. It is possible to over-tighten the adjustable cup. If you feel resistance when you turn the handlebars, this may be the case.

Raising the Handlebars

On some bikes, you may want to lower or raise the height of the handlebars to be comfortable. Actually it is the stem, which the handlebars are attached to, that is raised or lowered.

To adjust the height of your bike's stem, loosen the stem bolt, also known as the expander bolt, about four turns. Raise or lower the stem as desired, and then retighten the stem bolt. Make sure the handlebars are straight and be sure to tighten the stem bolt adequately.

It may be necessary to hit the top of the stem nut with a rubber mallet (after you loosen the stem bolt) to free the wedge or cone holding the stem in place before you can raise or lower the stem. If this is the case, raise the wheel off the ground, support the handlebars, and lightly hit the top of the stem bolt to free the wedge. Raise or lower the stem, and then tighten the stem bolt.

ADJUSTING THE HUBS

The hubs on your bike's wheel may need to be adjusted once in a while. A wheel that develops a "wobble" and seems loose is a sign that the cones on your hubs need tightening.

You will need two cone wrenches to adjust the hubs, because anytime you tighten or loosen one side of the hub, you'll need to hold the other side still with the second wrench.

To adjust the hubs, first remove the wheel from the bike. On most bikes, each side of the hubs has a locknut, a washer, and a cone that holds the bearings in place.

Loosen the locknut with a six-inch crescent wrench until you have access to the cone. Tighten the cone until the axle is firm against the bearings, then retighten the locknut.

If you want to overhaul the hub completely, remove the locknut, washer, and cone from the axle. Next, remove the axle from the hub (and bearings if possible). Clean all the parts in solvent and dry them. Finally, regrease the axle and bearings with bearing grease and reassemble.

SPOKES

Occasionally, you will need to tighten the spokes on your bike. How tight a spoke should be can only be learned from experience. Basically, if you find a spoke that is loose, tighten it until it has the same amount of resistance the other spokes in the wheel have.

To replace a spoke, you must first take off the tire, inner tube, and rim strip, then screw the spoke into the nipple in the rim. It's a good idea to carry a spoke wrench and an extra spoke with you on the road if you are going out for a few days.

Truing a wheel is done if the wheel becomes out of alignment. As various spokes in the wheel become loose, parts of the rim begin to bulge to one side or the other. The result is an unbalanced wheel that wobbles.

The remedy is to put the wheel in a truing stand and tighten or loosen spokes as needed until the wheel is true. Truing a wheel isn't difficult, but it can take time and requires patience. If you don't want to put the time into it, have a bike shop do it for you.

ADJUSTING THE BOTTOM BRACKET

If you "feel" any type of vibration when you pedal, the bottom bracket probably needs to be adjusted.

First, loosen the lock ring with a pin wrench. Then tighten the fixed cup with a pin wrench and retighten the lock ring. If you want to clean the spindle (the bottom bracket's axle that the pedal crank arms are attached to), you will need to remove the crank arms first, using the appropriate crank extractor tool. Then remove the adjustable cup and the bearings that are underneath it and pull the spindle out. Clean and lubricate all parts and then reassemble.

BRAKE PROBLEMS

Brakes can be adjusted with the *barrel adjusters* located on the brake cables. Move the brake pads farther apart or closer together by twisting the barrel adjuster until you get the desired spacing.

If the barrel adjuster is all the way out, you will need to adjust the length of the cable. First, loosen the bolt on the brake that holds the cable in place. Use needle nose pliers to pull the cable into the desired position and retighten the bolt. Use a third hand brake tool to hold the brake arms in place while you make the adjustment.

Most brakes also have a positioning screw—usually located on the top of the brake—which moves both brake pads to the left or the right.

FINISH LINE PRODUCTS

A key to keeping your bike running smoothly is to keep it clean and well lubricated. Dirt and grease on the chain, cogs,

MAINTENANCE AND REPAIR **143**

It's important to remove dirt and grease from your bike's chain periodically to keep it running efficiently. Finish Line's chain degreaser is an excellent tool for the job.

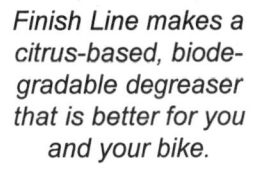

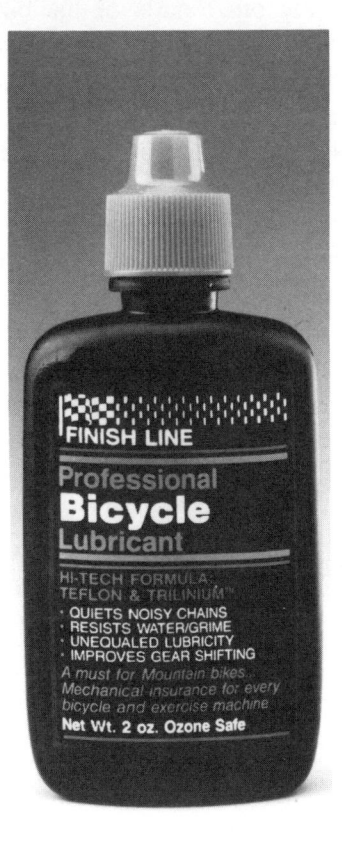

Finish Line makes a citrus-based, biodegradable degreaser that is better for you and your bike.

Only use a lubricant that is designed to be used on bikes.

Use a polish that is designed for bikes to protect your bike's paint job.

and derailleur will quickly begin to affect your bike's performance.

Finish Line Products specializes in products designed to clean and lubricate bikes. I use the following products and consider them extremely useful.

A Chain Cleaner is needed to degrease your bike's chain periodically. A chain cleaner is quick and easy to use and costs about $25. The chain cleaner is reusable, and you can buy additional liquid degreaser.

A clean chain will last longer and run quieter than a chain that is coated with dirt and other contaminants. Keeping the chain clean helps to prevent dirt from getting into the bike's sprockets and derailleur.

While you are cleaning the chain, also use some degreaser to remove grease from the derailleur, cogs, rear wheel, chain ring, and any other parts of the bike that have accumulated grease. Ever notice that the bikes used by racers are clean and dirt free? Bikes operate much more efficiently when they are not clogged up with dirt.

Consider getting a sprocket brush to clean grime out from between the rear sprockets.

Once the drive chain has been degreased, the next step is apply a fresh lubricant to the chain. Finish Line makes a variety of lubricants specifically designed for cycling. I've been using their *Synthetic Century Lubricant* with excellent results.

To clean the bike's frame, use a solvent that is specifically designed for bikes. Using the wrong type of solvent might damage your bike's finish ... and a new paint job is expensive.

For information about Finish Line Products, contact:

Finish Line Technologies, Inc.
19 Beach Street
Islip, NY 11751
(516) 581-2000
FAX: (516) 581-2012

10

Touring

What could be more enjoyable than seeing a new country or state while traveling its backroads by bike? Motorists generally stick to the well-known highways; cyclists travel the lesser known, but more scenic, backroads. Bicycle touring allows you to see new places up close and at a relaxed pace, rather than flying by them at sixty miles an hour in a car.

Bicycle touring also gives you the opportunity to enjoy being outside in the fresh air. Are you feeling a little burned out from work? I guarantee that a bicycle touring vacation will go a long way towards reviving you. What could be more relaxing than a leisurely ride through the wine country of northern California? Bicycle touring is an ideal way to unwind if you are feeling stressed out from life and work.

Going on a bike trip doesn't have to be expensive. In fact, you don't even need to own your own bike. Cost wise, there is something for every budget. From a little over $100 a week to expensive international tours to rarely traveled countries, you will most likely find something that's ideal for you.

TYPES OF TOURS

Bicycle touring can be divided into two basic categories: (1) tours that are booked through cycling touring companies, and (2) tours you organize and support yourself.

Going on an organized tour frees you from having to plan out a route, plot daily distances, and deal with accommodations. Conversely, going solo can be a lot of fun, too. Having the freedom to take any road you choose — at any pace you choose — can be very enjoyable. Another reason to plan your own trip is that you may want to go out on the road for an extended amount of time ... perhaps across a country over a three-month period. For a trip of this nature, you will need to do your own organizing.

A tour that offers full support will be able to provide you with complete repair services, especially if you rent one of their bikes.

Vacationing cyclists take a break after lunch.

Touring with a group is a great way to make new friends.

SELECTING A TOUR

Before you book a tour, there are a few decisions you need to make. There are also a few things you should look into to ensure you get what you pay for. For example:

How much support do they provide? How much support do you want? This is one of the first questions you need to ask yourself before picking a tour. Some touring companies offer extremely luxurious tours that take care of everything for you. Others offer very little.

Fully supported tours offer the convenience of worry-free touring. Hotels are prearranged and a van transports your luggage for you each morning to the next hotel. Lunches are laid out at designated locations—you simply show up and eat.

A big advantage to a fully supported tour is the quality of roadside service they should offer. On a recent Backroads trip I was on, tour leader Ann Mania was extremely helpful when it came to repairs in the field. Ann rode her bike while another leader drove the van. If Ann didn't have what you needed on her bike, the van was usually only a few minutes away. This type of support also lets you ride without having to carry spare parts, tools, and luggage on your bike. Even cameras, snacks, and extra water can be carried by the support wagon.

Having the option of not riding is another advantage to a supported tour. Don't want to ride the six-mile section of hills today? No problem—get in the van (also known as the "sag wagon").

Tours that involve lots of prearranged hotels and restaurants are expensive. If you want to save money, take a look at a camping tour. Backroads, for example, frequently offers the same tour in both camping and hotel versions. The camping tour has the same amount of roadside support, but is less expensive without the cost of lodging.

Camping tours are also a lot of fun. Many bike tours take place in some of the most beautiful outdoor areas on the planet. If you are going to ride through the Canadian Rockies, why not camp out and get the full outdoor experience? The disadvantage is that you are sometimes giving up luxuries such as hot water, etc., which is a consideration after riding a bike all day.

The disadvantage to the fully supported tour is cost. You can save a lot of money by taking a tour with minimal support. A week on a Backroads trip can easily cost you over $1,000. A week on a minimally supported tour might cost only $150.

A minimally supported tour might only supply you with a basic map, some luggage transportation, very basic roadside support (such as fixing a flat), a campsite, and leave meals up to you. The advantage to this type of situation is low cost. These types of tours are also fun because they generally are fairly large and social.

Keep in mind that a basic tour might not have as detailed route instructions as a fully supported tour. Also, if you get lost, you are probably on your own.

Has someone in the office done the tour? When you call the company offering the tour, ask if they've done the tour before. Also ask if one of the leaders you are going with has done the tour before. This is really important if the trip takes place in another country. You don't want to be waiting around while they iron out the various bugs that are almost always encountered the first time a tour is run. If it's the first time they are running the trip, you might want to pass.

Types of accommodations. Campsites or hotels? Single rooms or double occupancy? Air conditioning? What are the meals and are the meals included in the price? By asking a few questions before booking, you can avoid disappointment later. I once went on a tour that advertised "all meals included," and they were ... if you were a rabbit. Breakfast was a pile of apples and juice, lunch consisted of nuts and berries, dinner was a choice of peanut butter sandwiches or more apples. Naturally, we started eating out twice a day, which was fun, too. It wasn't fun, however, for people on the tour who hadn't budgeted for the extra expenses, thinking that three meals a day designed for hungry cyclists were included in the cost of the tour. Ask the same types of questions about the hotel rooms. Does your room have its own bathroom? Are there telephones? Is there a TV? Of course, some hotels and inns are terrific and don't have telephones and TVs, which is great unless you planned on having a phone.

Generally, with a reputable company, these types of questions will (should be) stated in their catalog. If you don't see it, however, don't assume—ask.

Terrain and distance. My friend Justin loves to tell novice cyclists, "Don't worry, it's flat and short." Then he takes them on a fifty-mile ride that features two eight-mile, six-percent-grade hills. He did this to me a few years back when I went on my first weekend tour with him.

"It's just a bump in the road," he smiled, when I asked him about the hill going up Pacific Coast Highway. "I promise you it's nothing to worry about." Needless to say, it was basically a paved cliff.

Justin rides by himself a lot these days. You definitely, however, don't want to pay for a tour that is way out of your league. Booking a tour that is within your ability is important. Be realistic—if you've only been riding forty miles a week on fairly flat terrain, don't pick a tour that covers 200 "rolling" miles. You won't have fun.

Get in shape for the tour. Don't go on a tour to get in shape, because it won't work. You are not going to get in shape in a week. In fact, if you overdo it, you may injure yourself.

If the tour covers 120 miles in a week, work your weekly mileage up to 100 miles a week for a few weeks before your trip. This way, you will be able to really enjoy your vacation, rather than have it turn into a week-long test of endurance and determination.

Same thing with the type of terrain covered on the trip. You don't want to "discover" the many hills on a trip when you're on them. Ask some questions when you call if the information is not in the company's catalog. Most of the major companies list each trip's "degree of difficulty" in their catalog. If they don't, it may be an indication that they haven't done the tour before.

What is the company's reputation? Most of the major bicycle touring companies are well known in the cycling industry.

A few phone calls to a local bike shop is usually all it takes to learn what a company's reputation is. Another good resource is the various cycling magazines. If no one has heard of them, you may want to pass on one of their trips. There are too many well established companies to choose from to risk an unheard-of company.

You can tell a lot about a company from its catalog and trip confirmation package. Check out a Backroads catalog as an example. You can obtain one by writing or calling:

Backroads
1516 5th Street
Suite Q323
Berkeley, CA 94710-1740
(800) BIKE TRIP
(800) 245-3874
(415) 527-1555 (in CA)
FAX: (415) 527-1444

Another question to ask in this regard is: *How long have they been in business?* It's probably a good idea to stay away from operations that are just getting started. Once again, there are too many well-established, well-known operators out there. Why take chances with an unknown?

What is the cost? In addition to the obvious costs, inquire about possible "hidden costs," such as transportation from the airport to the tour's starting location. If you need to rent a bike, it's going to cost something. Are you expected to pay for any meals or hotels? Are there any other transportation costs? Are there any "tours within the tour" that you will be charged for?

Quite often, additional costs are optional, such as for a side tour through a local winery. However, you may want to obtain all of this type of information before signing up. The cost of the tour may only include the bare essentials—or it may cover every expense encountered. The only way to be sure is to ask up-front.

SHOULD YOU RENT A BIKE?

Generally, on a fully supported tour, it's better to rent one of the tour company's bikes. By using one of their bikes, you will have the advantage of a basically endless supply of spare parts and quick repairs. For example, if you get a flat tire, the tour leader can swap wheels with you since she is riding on the

TOURING **151**

An afternoon tour through the old gold mining towns near the Silver Saddle Ranch and Club. Touring can be for only a few hours if you wish. Many people rent bikes and explore for a few hours when they visit a new place.

Generally, ride past the jail ... but don't stop.

same model bike as you. You keep on riding; the tour leader stays behind and repairs the flat. If the problem is more severe, such as a damaged derailleur, a new derailleur can be summoned from the support van.

If you choose to ride your own bike, you will probably need to stock up on your own spare parts. In addition, you will have to deal with the potential hassle of transporting your bike to and from the tour location.

However, if you own a nice bike and want to ride it on the tour, that is also understandable. You may feel it's worth it. Before you decide either way, take the time to check out what types of bikes the tour rents. You may be surprised at the quality.

HAVE FUN ON THE TRIP

A bike touring vacation should be fun. It's not a race. If you blast over the day's route at twenty-five miles an hour, you may be the first to finish, but you'll probably miss most of the sights. Part of the touring experience is the scenery and culture. Take the time to stop in the various small towns you may pass through. Visit the National Park scenic areas that may require a small side trip. Make a day of it.

Too often, novice cyclists get competitive with themselves on a tour. On a recent trip I took, a young couple flew over each day's route, often finishing in the early afternoon. They would spend the rest of their day in their hotel room wondering what to do. Each night at dinner we would ask, "Did you see the llama farm? Wasn't the view of the coast spectacular? Didn't you think the milkshakes in that town were amazing?"

Naturally, they had missed almost all of the sights ... but they had finished first. Don't let yourself fall into this trap. You're on vacation, so enjoy it!

As stated above, it's important to get in shape for the tour before you go. You probably won't have fun if you go on a trip that is beyond your current abilities. Use eighty percent as a guideline. If you can comfortably cover eighty percent of the trip's distance (over similar terrain) in your training rides, then you will most likely be able to handle the mileage and terrain of the tour.

PACE YOURSELF

It is important to pace yourself during your trip. You don't want to ride hard in the morning, and then run out of energy after lunch. The key is never to ride at 100 percent energy output. You want to pace yourself so that you will be able to ride the day's entire distance (if you want to). Hills are an area that may require "holding back."

WHAT YOU SHOULD BRING

It's possible to travel very light on a biking vacation. For a week-long tour, many cyclists only bring a few pairs of cycling shorts, jerseys, cycling shoes, and some clothes to wear after biking. Where you are going, how much support you will have, and the time of year will all dictate what you bring and how much you bring. Some of the items you may need are:

Cycling Shorts: A must bring item. I usually bring about four pairs, but that's by no means a rule. Many vacationing cyclists bring a different pair for every day of riding ... while my friend Justin brings one pair for the entire trip, which he washes every night.

Jerseys: If you are a novice and trying to save money, you can get by with T-shirts. However, most cyclists view cycling jerseys as must-bring items. I suggest bringing the same number of jerseys as shorts.

Cycling Tights: If you are going to be riding in cold weather, you may want to bring a couple of pairs of cycling tights. I've never felt a need for them, but then again, I never ride in very cold weather. Some cyclists prefer tights to shorts since the tights keep your muscles warm.

Shoes: Once again, if you are trying to cut costs, it is possible to go cycling with running or sport shoes. However, you will have an easier time if you bring a pair of cycling shoes. I consider this a must-bring item, although it's common to see vacationers pedal in running shoes. One pair of cycling shoes is generally sufficient.

Socks: Bring lots of socks unless you like doing wash. You will go through them faster on a cycling trip because you'll use two pairs a day.

Keep in mind that it may not be possible to use a hotel's laundry service since you will usually only be staying one night at any given location, and you will often be leaving fairly early in the day. Any washing of clothes you do will probably take place in the bathroom sink.

Clipless Pedals: If you own a pair of clipless pedals, bring them. The tour leader can easily put them on your rental bike, and you will probably enjoy having them if that is what you're used to. Keep in mind that you'll also need to bring your cycling shoes and matching cleats.

It may be possible to get a rental bike that already has clipless pedals identical to what you own, eliminating the need to bring yours.

Windbreaker: A must-bring item. Even if you go on a trip in the middle of summer, there will still be some cold mornings when you'll need to wear something over your jersey.

A lightweight windbreaker is ideal since it can be carried on your bike, yet doesn't add any meaningful weight. Get one that has holes in it (usually around the armpits) to let sweat escape. Most of the lightweight windbreakers are waterproof, and you will become fairly wet with perspiration if there isn't some means for the moisture to escape.

Look for one that also has a rolled-up hood in the collar. This way if it rains, the windbreaker can also be used to keep you dry. The hood is also useful when it is foggy, such as on early morning coastal rides, since you can become completely soaked in a short period of time.

Gloves: You will appreciate having gloves if you fall off your bike since they will help keep the skin on your hands. Gloves will also help prevent blisters if the bike's handlebars aren't padded.

Helmet: You should always ride with a helmet. In fact, most touring groups won't let you ride without one. Odds are that you will be supplied with a helmet, but you may opt to bring your own if you like the fit of your own helmet or don't want to wear a rental.

You may also want to get a visor put on your helmet to protect your face from sunburn.

Sunglasses: Like a helmet, sunglasses should be considered essential safety equipment. You may want to bring two pairs and an additional clear lens for overcast days. If you lose or break your glasses on the trip, it may be hard to find a replacement pair of cycling glasses, at which point you will appreciate having a backup pair.

Rain Gear: Rain gear consists of waterproof pants and a jacket. Go with the lightweight "shell only" type of clothing. The purpose of the rain gear is to keep you dry. In most cases, physical exertion will keep you warm. Also, the lightweight clothing won't add any noticeable weight on the bike.

If you are going on a fully supported tour, you may opt not to bring rain gear. Of course, this is totally dependent on where you are going. I never bring it, but I rarely go anywhere it rains

Participants in one of America's first organized bicycle tours lined up with their Ordinaires on the road outside Readville, Massachusetts on September 11, 1879.

much, and I'm usually on a well-supported tour. However, many cyclists don't leave home without it, and all the tour groups recommend bringing rain gear.

Other Clothing: Naturally, you will need "normal" clothes to wear when you are not riding. What you bring and how much you bring is related to where you go. For the most part, casual wear is the norm. If you're on a camping tour, you will need outdoor clothing for warmth at night. A visit to a local outdoor/camping store will give you an idea of what is available.

If you are carrying your clothes on your bike, weight is a big consideration. Look for clothing that can do double, or even triple, duty. If your luggage is being shuttled by van, you can be less choosy about what you bring. Generally, however, light packing is suggested.

First-Aid Kit: Optional if you have support—important if you are facing the road alone. Don't forget also to bring any medication you may require. It's often hard to find pharmacies in some of the locations a bike tour might take you.

To be better prepared should an accident happen, you might want to look into taking a general first-aid class through the American Red Cross. Learning how to deal with things such as a fractured bone or severe bleeding can become lifesaving knowledge should you, or someone you are traveling with, have an accident. Keep in mind that you may be alone when you are hurt—especially if you are mountain biking. Even if there is support nearby, you may still have to treat yourself until help arrives.

Sleeping Bag: Only a consideration (usually) if you are camping. I recommend you spend some time choosing a sleeping bag. You will quickly come to appreciate how annoying an uncomfortable sleeping bag can become if it prevents you from getting adequate rest after a long day's ride. One of the most common mistakes is getting a bag that is too small.

Some excellent sleeping bags are tapered and fairly narrow around the feet. The reason for this design is warmth; it takes less energy to heat the smaller area. However, most cycling tours don't take place in extremely cold climates. You want a sleeping bag that is roomy enough to be comfortable.

Sleeping bags are often provided on camping tours. If so, find out as much as you can about the sleeping bags they provide before the tour. For example, don't assume the bags are cleaned between tours—ask. You may opt to bring your own sleeping bag.

Ground Mat: A ground mat goes between your sleeping bag and the ground. It is made of foam, is inexpensive, and can make your outdoor nights a lot more comfortable. If a ground mat isn't provided, bring one.

Tent: Tents are almost always provided on an organized tour. If you are touring alone and want to bring a tent, you're in luck. There is a wide selection of very light and portable tents to choose from.

Flashlight: An essential item if you are camping. You also should bring an extra set of batteries.

Sunscreen: It's a well-known fact that the sun's rays are directly related to skin cancer. The fact that the ozone layer, which filters out some of the sun's harmful rays, has been thinned increases the risk of cancer from overexposure to the sun.

You will spend a lot of time outdoors on a tour, so it's important to use sunscreen every day to protect your skin. Bring whatever sunscreen you need with you, since it may be impossible to get if you travel to a remote location.

Hat: Wearing a hat with a visor is an excellent way to protect your face from the sun when you are off the bike. A baseball cap is ideal because it's lightweight, easy to pack, and inexpensive.

Day Pack: A day pack is a useful thing to have on any vacation. You can carry your camera, money, hotel keys, and any other items you may need. Keep in mind that you won't always be bike riding on your trip. You may want to go on hikes or explore the town where you are staying the night. A day pack is ideal for these activities.

Handlebar Bag: Rental touring bikes usually come with some type of handlebar bag, usually with a clear map bag on top so you can read directions without stopping. If you are using your own bike, you'll find a bag of this type to be very useful. Items that may be needed during the ride can be kept in the bag where they will be readily available.

Rear Rack: You will also want to put a rear rack on your bike. Even if you are not camping, the rack is a useful place to strap extra clothing and other items. A large variety of saddlebags can be attached to your bike to increase cargo space.

Passport, Wallet, Credit Cards, Money: Yes, it sounds obvious, but lots of people forget. I know of more than one traveler who has forgotten one or more of the items on this list.

Camera: It's surprising how many times I've heard people say, "I wish I'd brought my camera." If you own a camera, bring it. Be sure to bring enough film, batteries, and any other accessories you might need also. Odds are, you will be glad you have it if a large animal walks out of the woods to join you for lunch.

TOOLS AND SPARE PARTS

If you are touring without support, you must bring a tool kit and a few spare parts. With a fully supported tour, you probably don't need to bring anything. In most cases, the tour leaders will supply you with a patch kit if you want to carry one and will take care of any problems you or your bike may have.

If you are going on a partially supported tour, I would still bring at least a few basic tools and parts. Some of the items you should consider for a well-equipped tool kit in the field are: a Y wrench, a set of allen wrenches, screwdrivers (both slot and Phillips), a spoke wrench, an extra spoke, a chain rivet extractor, an extra chain link or two, a six-inch crescent wrench, a cone wrench (or two), a tire iron, a patch kit, a spare inner tube, a third hand (brake tool), extra brake and derailleur cables, and a pair of needle nose pliers. (For a description of what these tools are used for, refer to Chapter 9.)

With the above mentioned list, you will be able to repair

and adjust the most common problems encountered. Naturally, you should make sure your bike is as well tuned as possible before you hit the road.

If you have self-supplied van support, you can carry a complete workshop. Some cyclists go out on self-organized tours with van support and carry an extra bike and enough spare parts and tools to completely rebuild one or two bikes.

TRAVEL INSURANCE

Nothing is worse than having to cancel a vacation because of illness or an unforeseen event. You will be really annoyed if you can't get your money back. Buying travel insurance eliminates this concern since you will be reimbursed for the cost of the trip if you, or any of the agencies you are dealing with, cancel for any reason.

The agencies that supply the insurance usually also include various types of medical insurance, which is a good idea, especially for medical evacuation, which can be quite costly if you have to be transported by helicopter.

If you are planning to tour remote regions of the world, you want to be a little more prepared than for a local trip. For information about trip insurance, contact:

Tele-Trip Company
3201 Farnam Street
P.O. Box 31685
Omaha, NE 68131-0618
(800) 368-7878

THE PAC TOUR

Perhaps the greatest tour of all—and the toughest—is the Transcontinental PAC Tour (Pacific-Atlantic Cycling Tour). The tour covers approximately 3,350 miles over twenty-four days and gives riders the opportunity literally to ride across America. If you are looking for the ultimate cycling tour vacation, you might want to consider signing up for a PAC Tour.

PAC Tours aren't races (like the RAAM), but are designed for serious recreational cyclists who would like the opportunity to cross America at a realistic (a relative word) pace with full support. The tour supplies breakfast, snacks, lunch, lodging, gear shuttles, routing, and other types of tour support. Accommodations are usually in Best Western style motels, and single

Smiling faces prove that this twenty-four-day, 3,350-mile PAC tour is a lot of fun. (Photo courtesy of Lon Haldeman.)

rooms are available for an additional $500. Cost of the tour is about $2,500.

New versions of the tour are currently being organized. One of the tour's directors, Lon Haldeman, is planning both a southern and a northern route for future tours in order to give returning participants a different experience. In addition, some smaller tours are being put together, such as the "The Ridge of the Rockies" tour, which covers a 1,400-mile loop of the Colorado and New Mexico mountains, with the shortest day being eighty miles and the longest being 130 miles.

Could you ride a PAC Tour? Well, according to Lon Haldeman, cyclists should be fit enough to ride a fourteen-hour double century (200 miles). The average age of PAC Tour participants is forty years old (riders' ages have ranged from fourteen to sixty-four), the average speed is fifteen mph, and the average day is about ten hours.

Keep in mind that most participants plan months ahead for the tour and begin a training program to prepare. Lon Haldeman's training guidelines to prepare for a PAC Tour are included in Chapter 6 in the section on endurance training.

For further information about the PAC tour, contact:

PAC Tour
P.O. Box 73
Harvard, IL 60033
(815) 943-3171

11
Publications & Organizations

Magazines are an excellent source of up-to-date information about what is going on in the world of cycling. Bike riders are lucky—there are a lot of great magazines published about cycling. Some of the more popular are:

Bicycling

Bicycling is the biggest and (in my opinion) the best of all the cycling publications. *Bicycling* offers cycling enthusiasts a little of everything. What's nice about the magazine is that all subjects are treated thoroughly. Riding technique, nutrition, tour reviews, maintenance and repair, personality profiles, pro tips, equipment reviews, racing, and recreational rides are all well covered. Another plus to *Bicycling* is the excellent photography and graphics. Cost is about $20 for a one-year subscription.

Mountain Bike magazine, which is incorporated into the back of *Bicycling* magazine, is available for an additional cost of $10 to *Bicycling* subscribers. *Mountain Bike* is devoted entirely to mountain biking and covers equipment reviews, riding technique, tours, competition, first aid, and other information pertinent to mountain biking. For subscription information about both magazines, contact:

Bicycling
P.O. Box 7566
Red Oak, IA 51591-2566
(800) 666-2806

Bicycle Guide

Bicycle Guide magazine is a solid combination of equipment reviews, riding techniques, race updates, fun ride reviews, historical stories, nutrition, maintenance, and other information. *Bicycle Guide* deals with all types of bikes and cycling disciplines and features excellent photos. Cost is about $15 for a one-year subscription. For information, contact:

Bicycle Guide
P.O. Box 21130
Allentown, PA 18003-9928
(800) 456-6501

Velo News

Velo News, as is stated on its cover, is "The Journal of Competitive Cycling." Race reviews and previews, personality profiles, TV coverage reviews, racing technique, equipment reviews, and more are included in each issue. *Velo* deals with all aspects of competitive cycling, giving road, track, and off-road racing almost equal coverage. Cost is about $30 for a one-year subscription. For information, contact:

Velo News
P.O. Box 53397
Boulder, CO 80323-3397

Bicycle USA

Bicycle USA, as is stated on its cover, is the "Magazine of the League of American Wheelmen." The magazine deals with issues relating to The League of American Wheelmen (commonly referred to as LAW) and contains general interest articles about cycling.

LAW, which was founded in 1880 and currently has over 22,000 members, is an organization of bicyclists that provides information about the sport, protects the rights of cyclists, and sponsors events through a nationwide network of clubs and organizations. A subscription to *Bicycle USA* is included in the $25 LAW membership fee. For information, contact:

The League of American Wheelmen
190 West Ostend Street
Suite 120
Baltimore, MD 21230
(301) 539-3399
FAX: (301) 539-3496

Bicyclist

Bicyclist is the oldest cycling publication. The magazine deals with topics such as trade news, cycling laws, equipment reviews, riding skills, trade shows, and more. Cost for a one-year subscription is about $35 a year for the cycling industry and $75 a year for non-industry affiliated subscribers. For further information, contact:

Bicyclist
80 8th Avenue
New York, NY 10011
(212) 206-7230

Mountain Bike Action

Mountain Bike Action, as its name implies, is devoted entirely to off-road riding. There are lots of articles dealing with riding techniques, all of which are well written and informative. The magazine also gives examples of various training programs to achieve specific results. Other topics include: equipment reviews and previews, personality interviews, race information and reviews, and other topics of interest to off-road riders. Cost is about $20 a year. For information, contact:

Mountain Bike Action
P.O. Box 9502
Mission Hills, CA 91395-9963
(818) 365-6831

Mountain Biking

Mountain Biking is one of the cycling magazines published by Challenge Publications. Challenge Publications has a few different cycling magazines, so you may want to give them a call to see what is currently available.

Mountain Biking deals with new bike and product reviews, riding technique, competition, repair and maintenance, and other topics relating to off-road riding. Cost is about $28 a year. For further information, contact:

Mountain Biking
P.O. Box 16149
North Hollywood, CA 91606
(818) 760-8983

Triathlete

Triathlete deals with biking, swimming, and running, so it's not solely a cycling magazine. However, many of the topics covered in *Triathlete* are of interest to cyclists. Health and diet are particularly well covered.

Cyclists who get into cross-training may want to check out *Triathlete*. Cost is about $25 a year. For information, contact:

Triathlete
Winning International, Inc.
744 Roble Road, Suite 190
Allentown, PA 19103-9100
(215) 266-6893

BMX Plus

BMX Plus deals with BMX racing and related subjects. The action photographs in *BMX Plus* are excellent, showing lots of high jumps and freestyle action. Equipment reviews, race and event coverage, and technique are all well covered. For further information, contact:

BMX Plus
Daisey/Hi-Torque Publishing Co., Inc.
10600 Sepulveda Blvd.
Mission Hills, CA 91345
(818) 545-6012

Cycling USA

Cycling USA is the official publication of the U.S. Cycling Federation, which is the governing body for racing in the United States. *Cycling* features race coverage, personality profiles and interviews, and training. For further information about the U.S. Cycling Federation or *Cycling USA*, contact:

United States Cycling Federation

Cycling USA
1750 East Boulder Street
Colorado Springs, CO 80909
(719) 578-4581

BikeReport

Bikecentennial is an organization that supplies information and routes to cyclists planning tours cross-state, cross-country, or in other countries. Membership costs about $25 and includes a subscription to *BikeReport*, which features lots of information relating to bike touring. If you are planning on touring independently of an organized group, you will benefit from what Bikecentennial has to offer. For further information, contact:

Bikecentennial
P.O. Box 8308
Missoula, MT 59807
(406) 721-1776

PUBLICATIONS AND ORGANIZATIONS   165

This extensive collection of early bicycle lanterns is displayed at the Burgwardt Bicycle Museum. (Photo courtesy of Burgwardt Museum.)

The Burgwardt Bicycle Museum has over 200 cycles on display. (Photo courtesy of Burgwardt Museum.)

The Burgwardt Bicycle Museum

The Burgwardt Bicycle Museum, with a collection of over 200 cycles, is one of the best cycling museums in the country. It is also a great source of historical information about bicycling. For information about the museum, contact:

Burgwardt Bicycle Museum
3943 North Buffalo Road
Orchard, NY 14127-1841
(716) 662-3853
FAX: (716) 662-4594

Glossary

ATTACK—Accelerating during a race to pass another competitor or competitors.

BLOCKING—Getting in the way of other competitors to prevent them from chasing your teammate.

BONKING—Running out of energy. Also known as "hitting the wall."

BREAKAWAY—Accelerating ahead of the pack during a race.

CHASE GROUP—A group of riders who attempt to catch a breakaway.

CIRCUIT RACE—A multi-lap race.

CLINCHER TIRE—A tire with a wire or Kevlar bead that attaches onto the rim and has a separate inner tube.

CRITERIUM—A multi-lap race on a course about one mile long.

DERAILLEUR—A device that moves the chain from one gear to another.

DISK WHEEL—An aerodynamic wheel. Sometimes a spoked wheel with a cover.

DRAFTING—To ride in the slipstream of another rider.

DROP—To break away from another rider, as in "drop that rider."

ECHELON—Formation in which cyclists are in a staggered line with each rider downwind of and a little behind the rider in front.

FEED ZONE—An area along a course where food and drinks are handed to riders.

FIELD—The main pack of riders in a race.

FLYER—A lone rider who attacks.

FORCING THE PACE—To force the pack to ride faster by speeding up.

FRED—A novice or an inexperienced rider who acts foolish.

GAP—The amount of distance between two riders.

HAMMERING—To ride at 100 percent effort.

HONKING—Riding hard out of the saddle while holding onto the brake hoods.

HOOK — Slowing down so that your rear wheel touches a drafting rider's front wheel. Done by racers to discourage drafting.

INTERVAL — Riding hard and slow alternately. Used as a training technique as a way to drop weaker riders in a race.

JAM—Riding hard.

KICK—Suddenly speeding up to obtain a lead.

MASS START—A race in which all competitors start together.

MISS AND OUT—A velodrome race in which the last rider to complete each lap is eliminated until one rider is left.

NOODLE—To ride at a slow pace.

PACELINE—To ride in a line alternating the lead position.

POLE LINE—The top line on a velodrome, which is used to measure the length of the track.

PRIME—A race within a race for points or prizes.

PULL—Riding at the front of a group to break the wind.

SEWUP TIRE—A tire that has the inner tube sewn inside it. Sewup tires are one-piece units that are glued onto the rim.

SPIN—As in "to spin the pedals."

SQUIRREL—A rider who swerves a lot and is unable to ride in a straight line.

STAGE RACE—A race that takes place over several days.

TRACKSTAND—Balancing the bike in a stationary position

without removing your feet from the pedals.

VELODROME — A racing track for bicycles with banked turns.

Index

A

Accessories and custom equipment, 39-56
  aerobars, 56
    photos, 56
  bike racks and boxes, 50-4
    photos, 51, 52, 53
  children's seats and trailers, 55
    photo, 55
  clothing, 42-3, 45
  computers, 39-42
    photo, 40
  heart monitors, 46
  lights, 48-9
    photo, 48
  lightweight parts, 45-6
  locks, 47-8
    photo, 47
  protective gear, 50
  Rock Shox suspension, 49-50
  rollers and stationary trainers, 46-7
  timers and clocks, 40
  tire pumps, 44, 45
    photo, 44
  under-the-seat pouch, photo, 54
  water bottles, 45
Aerobars, 56
  photos, 56
Alkek Velodrome, 104
Alpenrose Velodrome, 104
American National Standards Institute, 59
Answer Products, 46
Avenir, 39, 59

B

Back problems, 116, 118
Backroads (tour company), 147, 150
Beach cruisers, 28-9

Bicycle, 88
Bicycle Guide, 161-2
Bicycle USA, 162
Bicycling, 11, 161
Bicyclist, 162-3
Bike racks and boxes, 50-4
  photos, 51, 52, 53
Bikecentennial, 164
BikeReport, 164
Bikes, 21-37, 76-7, 89
  anatomy of, 24-8
    bottom bracket, 27
    brake lever, 25
    chain, 26
    chain rings, 26
    chainstay, 26
    crankarms, 26
    down tube, 26
    fork, 25
    front brake, 25
    front derailleur, 27
    grips, 25
    head tube, 28
    headset, 25-6
    hub, 24-5
    pedals, 26
    photo, 24
    rear derailleur, 27
    rear dropout, 27
    rim, 24
    saddle, 26-7
    seat tube, 27
    seatpost, 27
    seatstay, 27
    spokes, 24
    stem, 25
    tires, 24
    top tube, 26
  choosing, 21, 23

Bikes, cont.
  cost, 23
  hybrid, photo, 22
  keeping in good condition, 76-7
  mountain, photo, 22
  off-road, photo, 22
  space shuttle, photo, 89
  tandem, photo, 22
  types of, 28-31
    beach cruisers, 28-9
    coaster brakes, 28
    hybrid, 30-1
    mountain, 29
    racing, 30
    recumbent cycles, 31
    road, 29-30
    tandem, 31
    touring, 30
    tricycles, 31
  what should you buy?, 31-2
    after-market compatibility, 31-2
    components, 31
    fit, 31
  why ride, 11, 13-4
Bio Sports, 120
BMX Plus, 164
BMX Stunt Bikes, 29
Bottom bracket, 27, 142
  adjusting, 142
Brakes, 25, 35, 142
  brake lever, 25
  front, 25
  maintenance and repair, 142
Burgwardt Bicycle Museum, 165, 166
  photos, 165

C

Cadence, 84
Chain, 26
Chain rings, 26
Chainstay, 26
Challenge Publications, 163
Children's seats and trailers, 55
  photo, 55
Clothing, 42-3, 45
  gloves, 43
  jerseys, 42
  rain gear, 43, 45
  shoes, 42-3
  shorts, 42

Coaster brakes, 28
Computers, 39-42
  altimeter, 41-2
  average speed, 41
  cadence, 41
  distance traveled, 40
  maximum speed, 41
  odometer, 40
  photo, 40
  speedometer, 39
  timers and clocks, 40
Cost of bike, 23
Crankarms, 26
Cross-trainer bikes, see Hybrid bikes
Cycling, history of, 14-9
  high bicycle, 18-9
  Hobby Horse, 14, 15, 17
  photos, 15, 16
  safety bicycle, 19
  velocipede, 17
Cycling USA, 164
Cyclists Touring Club, The, 18

D

Daisey/Hi-Torque Publishing Co., Inc., 164
Derailleur, 27, 137-9
  front, 27
  maintenance and repair, 137-9
    photos, 138
  rear, 27
Diet, 113-6, 122-3, 125-6
  carbohydrates, 123
  eating after riding, 123, 125
  eating on the bike, 125
  protein, 125-6
  water, 113-5
  weight loss, 115-6
Down tube, 26
Drafting, 97
Drais, Karl, 14
Draisienne, 14

E

Encino Velodrome, 103
Eyewear, 60

F

Feet, numb, 119
Finish Line Technologies, Inc., 144
Fork, 25

G
Grayson, Andy, 74
Grips, 25

H
Haldeman, Lon, 88, 159
Handlebars, adjusting, 140-1
Hands, numb, 118-9
Hazards, 121-2
Head tube, 28
Headset, 25-6, 140
  adjusting, 140
    photo, 140
Health, 115-6, 117, 118-9, 120-1
  back problems, 116, 118
  hygiene, 120-1
  knee pain, 120
  numb feet, 119
  numb hands, 118-9
  photos, 117
  saddle sores, 121
  weight loss, 115-6
Heart monitors, 46
Helmets, 57-60
  fit, 59
  photos, 58
  ventilation, 59-60
  weight, 60
High bicycle, 18-9, 95
  Ordinary, photos, 95
History of cycling, 14-9
  high bicycle, 18-9
  Hobby Horse, 14, 15, 17
  photos, 15, 16
  safety bicycle, 19
  velocipede, 17
Hobby Horse, 14, 15, 17
  photo, 15
Hub, 24-5, 139, 141
  adjusting, 141
    photo, 139
Hybrid bikes, 22, 30-1
  photo, 22
Hygiene, 120-1

I
Integrated Cycle Systems, 48

J
Journal of Applied Physiology, 123

K
Kish, Bob, 111
Knee pain, 120

L
League of American Wheelmen (LAW), 162
Lehigh County Velodrome, 103
Lights, 48-9, 61
  mounting, 49
  photos, 48, 49
  ruggedness, 49
  water resistance, 49
  weight, 49
Locks, 47-8
  photo, 47

M
MacMillan, Kirkpatrick, 17
Maintenance and repair, 127-44
  adjusting bottom bracket, 142
  adjusting hubs, 141
  brake problems, 142
  derailleur problems, 137-9
  photos, 138
  Finish Line Products, 142, 144
  fixing flat tire, 133-7
    photos, 134, 136
  photos, 127, 143
  spokes, 141-2
  steering problems, 140-1
    adjusting headset, 140
    raising handlebars, 140-1
  tools, 128-33
Major Taylor Velodrome, 103
Maney, Tom, 83
Mania, Ann, 147
Miller, W.H., photo, 15
Moore, James, 17
Mountain Bike, 161
Mountain Bike Action, 163
Mountain bikes, 22, 29
  photo, 22
Mountain Biking, 163

N
National Off-Road Bicycle Association (NORBA), 110
National Sports Center Velodrome, 103
NORBA (National Off-Road Bicycle Association), 110

NORBA News, 110

O
Oakley, 60
Off-road bike, photo, 22
Off-road racing, 108-10
   National Off-Road Bicycle Association (NORBA), 110
   starts, 109-10
Off-road riding skills, 67-77
   bunny hop, 72, 74
   descents, 67, 68
      photo, 68
   downhill braking, 68
   floating turn, 71
   front wheel lift, 70-1
   jumping, 72
      photos, 70, 73
   keeping bike in good condition, 76-7
   obstacles, 69-70
   picking a line, 69
   rear wheel lift, 71-2
      photo, 71
   spinning and traction, 75
   standing up, 76
   stationary hops, 74-5
   staying out of water, 77
   using speed, 69
   weighting and unweighting, 72
   Zen biking, 75-6
Ordinary bicycle, see High bicycle

P
PAC Tour, 88, 90-1, 158-9
   photo, 158
   training for, 90-1
Pacific-Atlantic Cycling Tour, see PAC Tour
Pedals, 26, 35-7
   clipless, 36-7
      photo, 36
   toe clips, 36
Peloton, 92-3, 106
   riding in, 106
   training for, 92-3
Penny Farthing, see High bicycle
Penseyres, Pete, 88
Profile, 56
Publications, 161-5

R
Race Across America (RAAM), 88, 111
Racing, 30, 94, 97-111
   bike, 30
   cyclists, photo, 94
   dealing with fear, 100
   off-road, 108-10
      National Off-Road Bicycle Association (NORBA), 110
      starts, 109-10
   photos, 98, 107
   previewing course, 99-100
   road, 104-8
      attacking and breaking away, 107-8
   start of race, 99
   velodrome, 100-4
      strategies, 102-3
      track bikes, 101-2
   wind resistance/drafting, 97
Rear dropout, 27
Recumbent cycles, 31
Reflective equipment, 60-1
Repair, see Maintenance and repair
Rim, 24
Road bike, 29-30, 77-9
   skills, 77-9
      riding up hills, 78-9
      turns, 77-8
Road racing, 104-8
   attacking and breaking away, 107-8
   riding in the peloton, 106
Rock Shox, 49-50
   suspension, 49-50
Rollers and stationary trainers, 46-7
Rover, 19

S
Sachs Bicycle Components, 34
Saddle sores, 121
Saddles, 26-7, 32-3
   anatomical, 33
   foam, 33
   gel seats, 32
   leather, 33
   liquid, 33
   racing saddles, 32-3
Safety, 57-66
   eyewear, 60, 64
   helmets, 57-60, 63

Safety, helmets, cont.
    fit, 59
    photos, 58
    ventilation, 59-60
    weight, 60
  how to ride safely, 62-6
    photos, 63, 64
  lights, 61
  protective pads and clothing, 62
  rearview mirror, 62
  reflective equipment, 60-1
    photo, 61
Safety bicycle, 19
Seat tube, 27
Seatpost, 27
Seatstay, 27
7-Eleven Velodrome, 103
Shifting systems, 33-5
  bar-ends shift levers, 35
  Campagnolo Ergopower™, 35
  down-tube levers, 34
  grip shifters, 34
  Sachs Power Grip, 34-5
  Shimano Dual Control™, 35
  thumb shifters, 34
Smith, George, 19
Snell, Pete, 59
Snell Memorial Foundation, The, 59
Spin Coach, photo, 83
Spokes, 24, 141-2
  maintenance and repair, 141-2
Steering problems, 140-1
Stem, 25

T

Tandem bikes, 22, 31
  photo, 22
Tele-Trip Company, 158
Tires, 24, 37, 44, 45, 133-7
  fixing flat, 133-7
    photos, 134, 136
  pumps, 44, 45
    photos, 44
Tools, 128-33
  allen wrenches, 131
  bike stand, 132
  cable cutters, 133
  chain rivet extractor, 128
  chain whips, 128
  cone wrenches, 131

Tools, cont.
  crank extractor, 133
  crescent and open-ended wrenches, 131
  fixed cup wrench, 133
  free wheel remover, 133
  lock ring spanner, 132
  needle nose pliers, 131-2
  photos, 129, 130
  pin wrench, 133
  screwdrivers, 132
  spoke wrench, 128
  third hand, 132
  tire irons, 131
  truing stand, 128
  Y wrench, 128, 131
Tour de France, 105
Touring, 30, 145-59
  bikes, 30
  PAC Tour, photo, 158
  pacing yourself, 152-3
  photos, 146, 147, 151, 155
  renting a bike, 150, 152
  selecting a tour, 147-50
  tools and spare parts, 157-8
  travel insurance, 158
  types of tours, 145
  what to bring, 153-7
Training, 81-95
  aerobic, 85
  avoiding redundancy, 91-2
  breathing, 93-4
  cadence, 84
  endurance, 88, 90-1
  for PAC Tour, 90-1
  for peloton, 92-3
  heart rate, 85
  intensity, 82-3
  intervals and sprinting, 85-6
  lactic acid, 84-5
  pacelines, 86
  photo, 87
  recovery rides, 87
  rest, 87
  setting goals, 93
  Spin Coach, photo, 83
  spinning, 83-4
  starting out, 81-2
  warming up, 82
Triathlete, 163-4

Tricycles, 31

U
United States Cycling Federation, 108

V
Velo News, 162
Velocipede, 16, 17
  photo, 16
Velodrome racing, 100-4
  strategies, 102-3

Velodrome racing, cont.
  track bikes, 101-2

W
Warming up, 82
Water, 113-5
Water bottles, 45
Weight loss, 115-6
Weinmann Sports, Inc., 46
Wind resistance, 97